ADVANCE PRAISE FOR *CRAZY-STRESSED*

"This book will save the sanity of parents and will save teens' lives . . . beautiful wisdom in straightforward language. This one raises the bar."

—Jodee Blanco, author of *New York Times* bestseller *Please Stop Laughing at Me: One Woman's Inspirational Story*

"For parents of today's teens, the world is not the one they knew as kids. The pressures on them to perform and compete are greater than ever; the virtual world has replaced the social everyday world with new plugged-in existences (Facebook, Twitter, Instagram, Pinterest, and more), as well as addictions to video games, and porn for guys. No wonder parents worry! To help parents navigate this challenging new millennium, Dr. Bradley draws on current research, clinical practice, and personal experience, offering parents practical solutions that will help their teens survive, thrive, and enjoy fuller lives."

—Philip Zimbardo, Ph.D., Professor Emeritus, Stanford University, and author of *Man Interrupted: Why Young Men Are Struggling and What We Can Do About It.*

Our teens are not crazy at all, they are reacting to a world sending confusing—even crazy at times—messages. Dr Bradley guides us through preparing them to deal with a far from perfect world while coaching us on how to better handle the occasional challenges our kids offer us. He makes learning effortless by seamlessly integrating relatable stories, science, and clinical

D0249716

expertise with humor. This book prepares you to build resilience in your children today so they'll become the adults we need to take over our world tomorrow.

—Kenneth Ginsburg MD MS Ed
Author of *Building Resilience in Children and Teens: Giving Kids Roots and Wings* and *Raising Kids to Thrive: Balancing Love with Expectations and Protection with Trust*

CRAZY-STRESSED

CRAZY-STRESSED

Saving Today's Overwhelmed Teens with
Love, Laughter, and the Science of Resilience

Michael J. Bradley, Ed.D.

AMACOM

AMERICAN MANAGEMENT ASSOCIATION

New York • Atlanta • Brussels • Chicago • Mexico City • San Francisco
Shanghai • Tokyo • Toronto • Washington, DC

Bulk discounts available. For details visit:
www.amacombooks.org/go/specialsales
Or contact special sales:
Phone: 800-250-5308
Email: specialsls@amanet.org
View all the AMACOM titles at: www.amacombooks.org

American Management Association: www.amanet.org

This publication is designed to provide accurate and authoritative information in regard to the subject matter covered. It is sold with the understanding that the publisher is not engaged in rendering legal, accounting, or other professional service. If legal advice or other expert assistance is required, the services of a competent professional person should be sought.

Library of Congress Cataloging-in-Publication Data

Names: Bradley, Michael J., 1951- author.
Title: Crazy-stressed : saving today's overwhelmed teens with love, laughter, and the science of resilience by / Michael J. Bradley, Ed.D.
Description: New York, NY : AMACOM, [2017]
Identifiers: LCCN 2016044192 (print) l LCCN 2017000499 (ebook) l ISBN 9780814438046 (pbk.) l ISBN 9780814438053 (eBook)
Subjects: LCSH: Parent and teenager. l Parenting. l Teenagers.
Classification: LCC HQ799.15 .B7268 2017 (print) l LCC HQ799.15 (ebook) l DDC
  306.874--dc23
LC record available at https://lccn.loc.gov/2016044192

In Memory of Virginia Smith-Harvey-Dawson.
To my kids Sarah and Ross: in different ways,
you each made me crazy! And you each also taught me
more about love than I ever could have imagined.
Thanks for the adventure.

ACKNOWLEDGMENTS

To those who have shaped my heart and so shaped my work, the best I can do is to say, "Thank you" to Bonnie Arena, Pete Bradley, Tony Chunn, Ginny Harvey-Dawson, Joe Ducette, Mattie Gershenfeld, Barry Kayes, Terry Longren, Father Michael McCarthy, Father John Riley, Pat Williams, Gene Stivers, and most of all, Chuck Schrader.

And to those who believed in this book and made it happen: Ellen Kadin, Marilyn Allen, and Sandy McWilliams. Thank you!

CONTENTS

PART III
Common Resilience Parenting Challenges:
The DOs and DON'Ts   161

PREFACE

Welcome to the most frustrating, satisfying, depressing, uplifting, infuriating, thrilling, sleep-depriving, and sometimes terrifying adventure of your life: parenting a new millennium teenager. My head knows a little about those feelings because I've spent more than three decades working with teens and parents. My heart knows even more about it because in the last 14 days I've experienced all of those emotions while parenting one of my own. Yesterday at 3 PM, as a result of a teen crisis in my family, I couldn't write. It was so bad that I asked my best friend, Cindy (another expert in adolescence, who also happens to be my wife), if this was the right time for me to be writing a parenting book. I told her that on the good days I feel I have something helpful to say to you, but on the bad days I don't. Cindy thought for a moment and then said, "Only write on the bad days. Parents will really connect with you then."

Cindy was reminding me of an upsetting thing we've noticed about many books on parenting teenagers. They are often filled with great information that enlightens our minds and yet depresses our souls, seeming to talk down to us, as if parenting was easy. These well-intended authors can also make it worse by telling us about their own "terrible teenagers" who ultimately get straight As in Ivy League colleges. They seem to think that sharing their own "Disney" endings will reassure us that everything will be OK. They forget to note that Ivy League scholarships are given to the children of about .0000015 percent of us real-world parents. We know that our real-world kids will get abducted by aliens before they win full rides to Princeton. So if we are having a hard time successfully parenting teens, is it perhaps because we're stupid?

Maggie, a client of mine, once made that point while walking into my office quoting from one such book: "This lady tells me that freaking out on my kid is a sign that my emotions are out of control." She angrily snapped the book closed. "As my daughter loves to say, 'Really! No, duh?' Dr. B, do you happen to know if this woman ever had a kid like mine?" A week earlier, Maggie's daughter had been dropped off at home at 1 AM from the back of a motorcycle, helmetless and smelling of beer. "I'd guess not," Maggie said. She continued, "Yelling comes automatically to me even though I know it's dumb. So I guess I'm 'beyond help' dumb, right?"

Maggie was not dumb, and neither are you nor I. It's just that parenting teenagers today can be really, really hard on your soul or heart or whatever you define as your essence or core being. It can challenge you in ways you've never been challenged in your life before, causing you to do things you already know are dumb. It can push powerful people to their knees, trying to figure out what the heck happened to them, as with another of my clients.

"I want you to know something about me," Jim said softly. "I spent 20 years in the Army. I did three combat tours, and I've been through things that most people think are the toughest things you could ever do." He leaned his weathered face forward, narrowed his eyes, and looked hard at me. "None of that ever made me feel as scared and crazy and helpless as I do trying to parent my 14-year-old daughter. I sh-t you not."

As I sighed and nodded in agreement, one of my old professor's mantras popped into my mind: *We are never in this world made more vulnerable than through the lives of our children.*

Some of those parenting books can sound as if they were written by the child-lottery winners—you know, the ones with the perfect kids who don't seem to know that they won that lottery. These are the experts who might work with troubled kids but whose worst personal parenting trauma was an unauthorized nose piercing. If a decorated nostril turns out to be their most terrifying teen trauma, then they really have no idea just how hard your job can be. Counseling troubled teens is *nothing* like parenting them. As you'll see in this book, that's a fact I know very well. I do both. I'm not overly impressed by couples who buy brand-new Corvettes or parents of perfect teens. But the folks who hands-on restore an abandoned '59 Vette, and the parents who never quit the fight for the soul of a challenging teen—those folks impress the hell out of me.

In fairness to those perfect world authors, most parents of teenagers (especially psychologist authors) rarely share the real deal with their casual peers. Sit in the stands at the high school soccer game and listen. The first parent offers, "Our Brendan has been accepted to the Johns Hopkins Summer Science program." "How wonderful," the second parent counters. "Our Susan is probably choosing the NYU course." If you could see their thought bubbles, Brendan's dad's might be ". . . but that all depends upon the judge's sentence for his threatening his girlfriend on Facebook." And Susan's mom's could well read ". . . unless we hospitalize her first for smoking weed every day." Most parents of struggling teens suffer quietly and alone, feeling like fools and failures, thinking that it's only their kids who screw up so badly. The controversial fact is that most teens are a little crazy, many are a lot crazy, and they all can make you crazy too.

My saying that teenagers are crazy does not make me popular at parties with my academic-type (versus hands-on-practice-type) peers. Many complain that my work portrays teens inaccurately and negatively, saying that I imply teens are mentally deranged and thus abnormal. This view, they argue, makes parents relate less well to them and damages their relationships. I answer that in one real sense, kids *are* deranged, but that's *normal* given their age, their poorly wired brains, and the over-the-edge world we've created for them. Adolescents can think and do things that are nuts and make decisions that don't seem to recognize reality. I argue that *not* facing up to that fact puts kids at great risk because we assume they can handle things they can't. If parents don't see their kids as somewhat nuts, it can destroy teen-parent relationships because parents will have failed expectations and will interpret crazy teen behaviors as personal attacks upon them. Worst of all, parents will be demoralized if the enormity of the parenting challenge is not acknowledged..

But I also see teenagers as wondrous. The same dictionary that defines "crazy" as meaning "deranged" adds other definitions— "extremely enthusiastic, passionate, infatuated, enamored"— and all of these words apply to teenagers as well as "crazy." They can also be creative, compassionate, insightful, and giving. They can be all of the great things that we prize in the world, and they do it as brain-challenged human beings under extreme stress, from which they are now terribly suffering at an unprecedented rate. That's why I also say that these people I call crazy are my heroes.

However, it is very easy to focus on the wonderful things in a teenager you don't have to live with. It's hard to remember the positives when it seems you are lurching from crisis to crisis, from loss to loss, from wound to wound, trying to recall why you ever wanted kids. W. C. Fields could have been talking about teenagers, not females, when he said they "are like elephants. I like to look at 'em, but I wouldn't want to own one."

If you already own one, this book might help you to enjoy the experience more. I can't promise you a Princeton University ending (and don't know I would if I could), but I do intend to give you some things far better: the skills you need to survive the bad times, the understanding to cherish the good, and the wisdom to help you shape a wonderful young adult you'll wish you could possess *a lot longer.* I promise you that can be true, no matter how difficult things might seem right now.

This is all gifted to you not by me but by other families. The insights and skills in this book are the nuggets of gold I have gathered in my three decades of witnessing the heroic journeys of families struggling through turbulent teen years. The vignettes I cite are actual stories from my case files, scenes I would scribble down after particularly powerful therapy sessions, hoping one day to share them. I have found they convey wisdom far better than my own words. (Note, though, that I have also given you some excerpts from my personal journal when I thought these would be helpful). Please accept these as war stories from veteran parents who already served their tours, offered to help you to survive your own.

What I don't need to give you as an owner of a teenager is the heart you need. You've already got that or you wouldn't be reading this book. As you'll see at the end of this journey of words, it is indeed the heart of the parent that is the most critical medicine in saving the life of a teen. It can help your heart stay sane if you remember that we don't really own these creatures. We're just leasing them for a short time that can often feel endless. Mother Nature or God (or whomever you like to blame) dropped these partially formed humans into our hands for caretaking while they complete the thrilling and often frightening journey to adulthood. Chronologically speaking, it isn't a very long time. But emotionally, like a deployed soldier's year, it can seem forever while you're there. So, like the soldier, use a calendar to remind you that you are on "short time," nearing the end of your parenting tour. That will help you keep your focus and discipline sharp, knowing that this will end one day. It will end, and surprisingly sooner than you think.

Remember when I said that parenting a new millennium teenager would be the most frustrating, satisfying, depressing, uplifting, infuriating, thrilling, sleep-depriving, and sometimes terrifying adventure of your life? It will be. It will also be the most important thing that you will ever do, and likely the thing that brings you the most peace when you one day review your life's adventures.

Buckle up, cadets! We're going in!

INTRODUCTION

Neuroscience has changed just about everything in our understanding of the game of adolescence. Since 1991, when Dr. Jay Giedd (while at the National Institute of Mental Health) first warned us that your teenager's brain doesn't work very well, other researchers have produced stunning insights into how adolescent brains work (and don't work), revolutionizing neurological understanding of adolescence. Yet in the decades that followed, we seemed to be unable to apply that knowledge to make much of a dent in the suffering of our kids. In fact, as you'll see shortly, life for them in many ways is the worst it's been in the roughly 50 years that we've been collecting good data on teenagers.

Jay predicted a few of the causes when writing the Foreword to my first book in 2002. He had no idea of how amazingly future-smart he would be when he said:

> While the biology of the teen brain probably hasn't changed much in the last few thousand years, the environment has changed tremendously. Teens today are faced with a dizzying array of choices, more potent and addictive drugs, and, through media and the Internet, far greater exposure to sexual material. Stone age impulses now have Computer Age temptations.[1]

That mix of neurology, technology, and culture has proved to be a scary stress recipe that has grown substantially more powerful since Jay first described it. Our Computer Age has indeed created enormously powerful cultural changes that occur with amazing speed, leading to unprecedented stresses for our teens. They are clearly suffering as a result. But those of us who love them can respond in equally powerful ways to save them. I'm here to help you do just that by integrating our knowledge of teen neurology with that of teen resilience—two sciences that woven together can create an amazing body armor to protect the hearts of your children from the threats of their world.

I use a lot of military metaphors in my writing, which is more a product of my parenting experiences than my Army ones. Like Jim (the client I quoted in the Preface), I've found parenting teenagers to be the more challenging adventure. I've also found that military training is very helpful in meeting my parenting challenges. No joke. Because when the stuff hits the fan, both soldiers and parents work much smarter and better when guided by a clear, carefully thought out *mission* (an ultimate goal) supported by smart *strategies* (subgoals to fulfill that mission) achieved with specific *tactics* (what to do when). For CEOs, soldiers, teachers, and especially parents, those three elements help us to replace reflexive, destructive, and dangerous reactions (such as slapping her face when she f--ks you off) with new ones that are amazingly more powerful (such as *walking away*—just trust me on that one for now).

This organizational model helps us override our built-in parenting instincts that in a nanosecond can convince us that hurting her for being hurtful will be satisfying and effective. The problem is that hurting her *can* feel satisfying and seem to be effective, but only for that nanosecond. In the next, it can cause crippling parental remorse. It can also lead to World War III. So using the military model to organize our parenting helps casualty rates to go way down and mission success rates to soar.

But have you ever really thought about exactly what your mission should be? Probably not, which is a little scary since everything else we do as parents should be directed by a mission designed to meet contemporary challenges. Thus, Part I of this book is about defining a clear, overriding parenting mission developed by reviewing critical information on the challenges facing new millennium adolescents. The data will dictate that goal. They will also help you to be empathetic with your kid, which is hard to do if you think you already know what it's like to be a teen in today's world. You don't. Even if you were a teen only 20 years ago, you still don't know. Having fewer facial wrinkles—that is, being relatively young—can even make you more inclined to screw things up because you assume that you do know your kid's experience, and then you further assume that you know exactly what your teen should do in those circumstances. Mother Nature bestows minor dementia upon the older among us so we're better able to say, "I forget what it's like to be a teenager. Please tell me." That turns out to be a very smart thing to say to your kid.

Part I of this book gives you a tour of teenagers' world, including the neuroscience of their brains (which often don't work so well), the astounding impact of their technology (which works all too well), and the crazy world around them (which works frighteningly well at promoting unwell behaviors). If scary movies are not your thing, perhaps you should not read Part I just before bedtime.

Part II gets hopeful. It starts by defining your critical strategies or subgoals—assets your kid needs not only to survive his adolescence but to flourish throughout it by building a near-magical skill called resilience, something we always find in teens who do well. Part II then supplies you with the specific tactics you need to accomplish those resilience-building strategies. The really wonderful news about resilience is that it is not just a genetic trait but rather something that can be built in all kids to lead them to wonderful lives in spite of temporary craziness. If you are focused only upon the goal of surviving your kid's teen years, be careful about shortchanging your aspirations *especially* in the tough times. If you ask little of yourself and your child, that's likely what you're going to get. Better to plan for the worst but work for the best. Resilience-focused parenting works really well for teens who are already doing well, but surprisingly to many, it works *even better for kids who are struggling terribly.*

Part III then puts it all together with down and dirty, what-to-do-when parenting suggestions—scripts that use the neurologic, cultural, and resilience science you'll get in earlier chapters to create smart resilience-building responses to the specific challenges that often cause explosions in families with teens. *But do not flip ahead to those chapters.* In the military, that would be like skipping boot camp to go directly to SEAL school. It ain't gonna work. You must understand the basic principles to skillfully use these tools, and more important, to tailor them to the challenges of your particular kid. That knowledge will give you the confidence and motivation you'll need to accomplish the most demanding and fulfilling job you'll ever do.

But there's one more thing you'll need. A clear mission, smart strategies, and powerful tactics mean nothing without that mystical energy called love to bind everything together with selfless, passionate power. If you ask the hero soldier why he risked his life, he typically won't talk mission. He'll quietly say that in the end, it all came down to saving the people next to him. The parents I know would also take a bullet without a thought to save their child. Winning the game of parenting a new millennium adolescent requires that the energy of love be smartly expressed with the training you'll get here. One without the other won't get it done. And you might be comforted to know that the strongest expression of parental love for a teenager is often not the soft, flowery fluff of movies, as this father learned the hard way:

Tom sighed heavily. He had just finished describing a terrifying week during which his 14-year-old daughter had twice disappeared into the night for several hours to do, as Tom described it, "God knows what with the devil knows who." Tears slowly rimmed his steely eyes. "I can't begin tell you what happens inside of me in the middle of the night, *in the middle of winter,* when she goes missing."

We sat in silence for a bit and then he continued. "Want to hear something weird? I thought I loved her when she was a little girl, before she got crazy. And then this week, I *hated* her for going crazy, and knew I would never forgive her for what she did to my wife and me. And when she finally came home last night, I *was* able to forgive her and even say . . ." He paused, swallowed hard, and then let his tears fall as his voice broke. "And even say that I loved her. Now I know that real love of a child is not the sweet, huggy-kissy kind. It's the hard, middle-of-the-night, I-will-hate-her-forever kind that gets tested, that pushes you way further than you ever thought you could go, only to find that in the end you still love her, even though you still want to kill her."

He paused to collect himself, then continued. "That night I wasn't sweet when I told her I loved her. When she screamed that I was a *'f--king lunatic,'* I screamed back, *'Want to know why*

I'm a f--king lunatic? Because I f--king love you! That's f--king why!'" Then Tom shook his head, sighed, and smiled a tired smile. "Believe it or not, we ended up hugging. Not pretty. But it worked."

Tom was right about what love frequently is when parenting your teen: It's often not pretty, but it always works.

Before we proceed, I need to confront you with one radical difference between the military and parenting. Military planning demands an exit strategy. In parenting, there can be no such idea. Your kid can quit on you, but you can never quit on your kid, no matter how much you want to at times. You must be in this for the duration. Your unwritten and sacred parental oath says that you are allowed to hate your kid's actions, but you are not allowed to hate your kid. You must vow to hold the high ground of unconditional parental love come hell or high water. In the worst of times, that unbreakable bond becomes a life preserver for your child when she flounders in terrifying seas. In parenting, retreat is not an option.

So if you're ready, turn the page and we'll start your tour of your teenager's world. You do know what they say about paranoia, right? Read on and find out.

CRAZY-STRESSED

PART I

The Anti-Adolescent Resilience Conspiracy

"It's not paranoia when they're really trying to kill you."

The endless stairs disappeared into the basement darkness like the entrance to hell. Our 13-year-old footsteps echoed in the huge empty space. *"Move it!"* barked our guard, a massive Sister of St. Joseph, a huge nun wearing a bizarre black outfit with a foot-tall headpiece—an image that would intimidate a terrorist today. Five of us sinners were being herded into the convent basement for a terrible punishment I can recall for some terrible crime I've forgotten. As our eyes adjusted a bit to the darkness, we were initially relieved to hear that we were not to be executed. Instead, she commanded, we were to *"Clean this basement as if your savior is coming to visit."* Our guard then smacked Billy Devaney on the head, twirled around, and vanished up the steps.

Billy, the funniest person I ever met, very likely had been the genius behind whatever sacrilege we had committed. Never known as a quitter, Billy immediately ran to a very dim corner of the basement and yelled, *"Holy sh-t!! The nuns got under-wear!!"* It was true! The answer to a blasphemous question we had never even pondered. Hanging on a clothesline was nun underwear! The garments were all black, some were enormous, and seeing them had to have been a mortal sin. Having nothing to loco (since a mortal sin means going directly to hell), Billy took down a huge bra, put it on, and stuffed the cups with other undies. *"They're gynormous,"* he yelled as he danced around the basement. *"Cup size B-52!!"*

Our fear and perverse sexual excitement exploded into screams of laughter as we watched Billy dance us all to Hades. Suddenly, he froze in place, his bugeyes even buggier than I had ever seen. He was staring at the steps as an enraged and athletic Sister of St. Joseph flew down, taking several stairs at a time with her habit hiked up to her knees. My memory is of an eight-foot-tall linebacker nun charging at a four-foot-tall, paralyzed Billy as his B-52 bra sagged sadly to the floor.

—From the author's personal journal

I share this ridiculous but true story since it supports the mission of Part I of this book—namely, helping you to understand a bit of what your adolescent is trying to survive, an experience very similar and yet very different from the one you recall. The parts that are the same have to do with the age-old bizarreness of adolescence, but you've probably forgotten that as a result of your middle-age parental senility. That disease rewrites our own true adolescent history with a PG-13 version in which we were all sane, industrious, and virtuous. But for both you and your kid, adolescence was/is a wild interactive mix of neurologically ("crazy") challenged brains, overwhelming sexual obsessions, intense envelope-pushing curiosity, and strange, angry adult creatures who do not seem to have a clue about what any of that is like. To a teen, it can feel like a conspiracy.

Years after that incident in the convent basement, at a gathering of that same group of boys (we made it out alive), we reminisced about that day and the beating that befell Billy. Eddie said, "You know, it always felt like they were out to kill us." Tony laughed, saying, "Man, you were always paranoid." Billy soberly responded, "It's not paranoia when they're really trying to kill you."

But some parts of today's teen experience are so painfully different from what we lived through that Billy's words ring truer for your kid in her world. By assuming that they deal with the world we recall, many of us adults see the typical millennial teen as over-indulged, self-centered, and lazy. I actually hold the contrary view and am amazed that so many of them do so well—certainly much better than my "gangster friends" (as my father lovingly called them) or I would have done had we grown up in their world. So many things have changed so radically that, taken together, they play like a sophisticated plot to destroy the resilience of our teens.

Chapter 1 argues this by taking a quick look at some scary 50-year comparisons that show how our teenagers are suffering at unprecedented rates. Chapter 2 addresses one huge cause of this phenomenon by explaining how the world around our kids has changed so radically from the one you recall from your own adolescent days. Chapter 3 looks at the neuroscience of the adolescent brain, a bubbling mass of developing wires ill-equipped to handle these types of threats, and then offers a great model to help you and your kid organize and understand adolescent brain function. Chapter 4 opens by describing how most of us adults are trying to help, largely by fighting this war with the lessons of the last one (our own adolescence), which is a mission that never succeeds. Finally, the chapter ties all of this together by offering a new mission statement developed from the intelligence gathered in the first four chapters, a mission I argue is the only tenable one to win the fight for the heart of your child.

So let's roll into Chapter 1 and upset you with how terribly our kids are suffering in comparison with prior generations of teens. By Chapter 4, I'm afraid that you might agree that Bugeyed Billy was right: It appears we *are* trying to kill them.

ONE

A Generational View of Teen Suffering

The Kids Are Not All Right

"My dad, he keeps sayin' I just got to toughen up and be like him, you know, like back in the day when the world was so much harder. He says kids today got it so easy. My mom, she just looks freaked out all the time, like she don't know what to say or do. My little brother, he's nine, he gets big eyes when he hears what I been through, like he don't want none of growing up." Fifteen-year-old Misty paused for a moment, looked up at me, and then continued. "I think my little brother is the only one who gets it."

Misty had just finished her second hospitalization in 12 months for suicide attempts.

Your Teen Years Were Nothing Like Your Kid's

If you think your teenager is more stressed, anxious, and depressed than you were back in your teen day, you're right. If you think that's because he's lazy and weak or she's self-centered and spoiled, you're wrong. Our kids are clearly suffering in unprecedented numbers—just exactly as we would have had we grown up in their world. Adolescent mental illnesses have exploded over the past 50 years to a point where the word *epidemic* fits. That view is supported by much more than just stories from overwhelmed mental health folks, and it's not the result of just "looking for it more."

Researchers such as Jean Twenge of San Diego State University and her peers have been comparing the teens of 50 years ago to those of this generation and have found some profound and scary differences. Anxiety and depression rates among teens are up 300 to 500 percent, as determined by comparing archived data from very reliable tests administered over those decades.[1]

Suicide rates have similarly ballooned to the point where for the last several years, every fifth to sixth kid strolling down the high school hallway either tried to end their lives or had a serious plan to get that done. This is new. Forty years ago, I recall having a vigorous teenage debate about the real meaning of Blue Oyster Cult's "Don't Fear the Reaper" (a song some interpret as being about teen suicide) since my "gangster friends" and I didn't understand what it was really about. Back then, we knew of no peers who tried or even mentioned suicide. Today, suicide is part and parcel of what teens deal with routinely, either themselves or with a close friend. Other 50-year comparison data show more changes that are also worrisome and likely related to those horrific disease numbers. You need to know these to know your kid.

"Who's Got Control of My Life?"

Today's teens feel less control over their lives, which is a very big deal. Over the decades, we've continually questioned kids about a life view called locus of control (LOC), which essentially asks them if they control the outcome of their own lives (internal LOC) or if their lives are driven by forces beyond their control (external LOC). Over 50 years, most adolescents have shifted from internal to external LOC, which is a really scary change.[2]

Teens with internal LOC feel more secure and confident about life since they believe they can pretty much make whatever they wish happen, even if they're doing poorly at the moment. Failing kids can say things such as "I'm just lazy" and "I can turn this around anytime I choose." Even when they're failing, internal LOC kids can feel in control. But external LOC teens can feel like a powerless, rudderless boat in an ocean storm, which is pretty much the prescription for anxiety and depression. That view can make life look bad and death look better.

While increased hopelessness is universal among teens today, the nature of that external LOC despair varies by socioeconomic class as a function of our current two-world economy (winners, losers, and a few folks in the middle). Watch some episodes of *The Wire* and you'll shut off your TV with a disturbing sense of the palpable despair of teens at the bottom of today's economic pile. Contemporary child poverty (which is also increasing) is absolutely soul crushing for kids today versus 50 years ago, and it involves a lot more loss than just financial. Back then there were many more factories and farms and places to go to earn enough to climb out of the 'hoods—jobs offering meaningful economic opportunities for those who were willing to work hard. There were also more critical supports such as spiritual centers, intact families, and positive adult role models. Those things have mostly disappeared with the jobs.

Many of these kids can't even qualify anymore to join the military, which back in the day was the last train out of hell for many of us. Studying the devastating quicksand of today's poverty has convinced me and most of my old "gangster friends" that we would have become true gangsters had we grown up in today's version of teen poverty. There often seems to be no other realistic option for survival, let alone feeding a family. Selling drugs to make a good living for the few short years you expect to live can make perfect sense in a horrific way.

Middle-class teens (the disappearing breed) face less brutal but very similar challenges. Bewildered parents of these teens speak of being trapped between two socioeconomic worlds: the scary world below reaching out to swallow their kids, and the unattainable one above, the one requiring admission tickets that often cost six figures (that is, college degrees).

The poor are not the only ones who are suffering. External LOC hopelessness is also killing those often entitled, super-high-achieving kids who appear to be on top of the world. It turns out the view from up there can look just as dark. It did to Frankie:

"I take three APs [difficult Advanced Placement high school courses that can lead to college credit], have a 3.75 GPA, play two sports, and am in the band and on student council. On a good night I sleep, maybe, four or five hours. Today, my college coach [a college adviser hired by his family] said to pretty much forget about getting into Princeton, Stanford, or MIT [universities he loves] since I don't have 'the right stuff.'" As

Frankie said "right stuff," he framed his exhausted head with quotation mark fingers.

"I've had no life since sixth grade, I work my freakin' ass off, and I can't even go to a college I want? I'm *done*, man. I quit. I mean, exactly what is the freakin' point of life if you have no shot to do what you want no matter how hard you try? You tell me again, man. Why *shouldn't* I smoke weed?" Tears were pooling in his eyes as hopelessness welled in his heart.

As Frankie spoke, I flashed back five decades to another discussion with my "gangster friends," in which we all spoke confidently about where we were going in life and how we could make those things happen if we just worked hard. I wished I could have promised Frankie it would work out for him as it had for us. All I could do honestly was listen.

"And What Is the Point of Life?"

A second 50-year teen comparison very much relates to Frankie's "freakin' point of life" question. It has to do with goals those generations set. Years ago, most adolescents spoke about making a difference in the world, of finding meaning and purpose in their lives. Science tells us that meaning and purpose are wonderful anti-depression and anti-anxiety treatments that are required for true happiness in life. Today's teens are more likely to say the point of existence is to acquire material goods. That philosophy could be viewed as another prescription to create depression and anxiety. As one 17-year-old succinctly put it, "He who dies with the most toys wins." I remember wondering where he might have gotten that inspiration (it's actually a quote attributed to Malcolm Forbes). A few weeks later, I read the words on the bumper of the Mercedes in front of me. It was driven by an adult. He did not look all that happy.

Not My Kid

A third comparison finding that may be related to the epidemics of teenage anxiety, depression, and suicide has to do with how we parents have largely decided that failure and even constructive criticism are toxic to our children. Parents of old tended to let their kids take the rap for their own bad behaviors with coaches, cops, and teachers. Old world parents would often unquestioningly add "other consequences" to those imposed by those authority figures (not a recommended tactic—we'll talk later). Today's parents are more inclined to "lawyer up" when those once respected authorities dare to criticize their little darlings. In my work as a forensic examiner, I once suggested a non-courtroom conflict resolution to a police officer trying to resolve a lawyered-up bullying conflict between two kids: "Maybe if you just informally visited her [the bully's] home and explained to her parents how hurtful her behavior has been?" I asked, adding, "Maybe they'll see the light?" He laughed sadly. "Where do you come from?" he asked. "You think anyone today respects police officers enough to care about what we think?"

Some Boredom Can Be Good

The fourth thing that's changed over time is time, or specifically how we allow teens to spend it. Most parents, rich or not, believe that the more we structure teen time, the safer and better off adolescents are. In particular, parents of teens with means tend to rush their kids from structured activity to structured activity, leaving precious little open time when teens must occupy themselves. While it is true that most bad teen things do happen away from adult supervision, teens learn more critical life skills when they structure their own time. It turns out that some boredom is extremely therapeutic and is often the energy of creation: "I'm soooo bored! I can't stand it! There's nothing to do!

But I guess I could start to write that script that's been rolling around in my head . . . " It is tricky finding a good mix of safe and productive nonstructured time, but for now know that most experts believe over-scheduling is another factor in the erosion of resilience and the consequent suffering we see in our kids. We likely have structured their lives so much to make them so smart that we're making them stupid, as one father told me:

Dr. Bradley, in your lecture when you spoke about how we may be disabling our kids with excessive caretaking, you struck a nerve. Last weekend my 20-year-old genius son called me at midnight from 100 miles away. He was up in the mountains with his friends driving my beloved Range Rover on a weekend trip. He's a smart kid, majoring in engineering and doing very well. "Dad, the tire is flat," he said. "It's got a nail in it. What do we do? There's no gas stations around here and it's like totally dark!"

He sounded panicked. I couldn't believe it. "For God's sake, just change it!" I said. "How do we do that?" he asked. So for an hour I had to calm him down and walk him through a simple tire change. None of his genius friends knew what to do either.

"The next morning after he got home, I went out to my Rover to get the tire repaired, but the tire and the wheel were not in the car. When I woke my son up to ask where my $700 worth of wheel and tire was, he was annoyed that I woke him to ask such a dumb question. 'I don't know, Dad. We were in some wild area. Couldn't tell you where. Why do you care? The tire was broken so we just left it there, right?' That's when it really hit me how much we parents knew at 20 that our kids do not. How the hell did that happen?"

"It *Is* All About Me"

A final factor about adolescents that's changed over the last few decades answers that nagging question in the back of your brain as you stare at your kid snapping 200 photos of herself: "Was I really that self-centered when I was her age?" The answer, according to psychologist Michele Borba's research, would be no, you were not.[3] Our kids are about 40 percent less empathetic and 60 percent more self-centered than those of 30 years ago (when we first began measuring this). This is not because they are morally inferior to us but because they've grown up in a culture that saturates them 24/7 with "It's all about me" messages. That is really bad news for teen resilience.

What used to be mocked as the "bleeding-heart/hippie" characteristic of caring has now been demonstrated to be perhaps the best predictor of success in life, far beyond SAT scores and Ivy League degrees. That "limp-wristed," empathetic, community-service kid ("I worry about those folks in the shelter. What can we do to help?") has far superior life success capabilities than the aggressive egocentric football hero ("Enough about me, babe;

let's talk about me"). It turns out that empathy breeds powerful achievement skills, including collaboration, problem solving, and creativity. Ask any CEO what she looks for when hiring staff. Football is a game. Empathy is the salvation of both our species and our children. Empathetic kids are less stressed, happier, and more resilient and successful.

So if you think that your teen seems so much more stressed, depressed, anxious, and self-centered and less resilient than you were at her age, know that you are not as dumb as she says you are. Mantras such as "20 is the old 16" are used by many teen experts when it comes to comparing generational maturity. In Parts II and III, we'll train you to begin to turn this around. But before we get to that, you need to know that your kid's stress/anxiety epidemic has a whole other world full of challenges that are making him crazy. That world would be his world. Turn the page and we'll do some exploring since this indeed is a new planet. You need new maps.

TWO

Contemporary Teen Culture

Their World Is Not All Right

The circles under Rhianna's 14-year-old eyes were startling for such a young girl. She looked too tired to talk. After a long awkward pause following my "What brings you here?" question, her dam burst: "*Everything!* Where do you want me to start?" As her phone buzzed nonstop with texts, she rolled her eyes and sighed. "Sorry. My phone is blowing up, *again*, with all the drama. I can't keep up with it. I forget who hates me and who likes me right now. Mostly they all hate me today. My schoolwork sucks; there's no way I can get into college. I can't pay attention since my brain is like spinning all the time. Besides, we [her family] can't afford it. BTW [by the way], who can? My parents are, like, exhausted and freaking out half the time, mostly about money, since we don't have any. My boyfriend, if he is still my boyfriend 'cause that's what these texts are about, he's like doing weed nonstop now. He's become this zombie-person. He might be doing pills. I can't sleep. I can't wake up. My stomach hurts a lot."

She paused for a breath, glanced at her buzzing phone screen, and then disgustedly threw it into the pillow next to her. "You know, I hate that thing, and I can't stop looking at it. [The messages are] mostly something that puts my stomach in a knot. It makes me feel like crap. It's killing me." She laughed a cynical laugh. "That's freaky. That's what my mom says about her cigarettes!"

As I wrote those notes after Rhianna's session, I tried to recall my own 14-year-old pressures that I thought were so bad at the time. Rhianna would think my 14-year-old world was a vacation, and likely yours as well. Think not? Let's take a little tour of teenage culture today and make a few stops to see what a resilience-shrinking/stress-growing world looks like.

Technology: Giving Nukes to Terrorists

Tech has changed everything about adolescence. Some changes are wonderful, such as providing 24/7 access to wonderful stuff. Some are terrible, such as providing equal access to terrible stuff. Both of these factor into teenagers' unprecedented sleep deprivation (as we'll discuss shortly). Remember the stressful parts of your own teen world? Tech has essentially provided nuclear weapons to those forces to exponentially increase the stressors on your kid. Examples?

■ **Social management.** Back in your day, how many kids' opinions of you mattered and had to be managed, and in how much detail? Your daughter, like some corporate PR exec, now must manage *10 times* more public perceptions and to incredible detail. Her privacy and peace of mind died the day the world's first text was sent. She must monitor and strategically respond to endless electronic postings about her every aspect among many more peers. You had the safety of time and distance since you could wait until the next day, after a good night's sleep, to even learn about the relatively few judgments being made about you. She can be up all night trying to do the impossible, namely managing the unmanageable electronically shared perceptions, opinions, and judgments of others. Attempting to do the undoable is another one of those classic recipes for anxiety, stress, and depression—and suicide.

Dylan looked completely spent, as would any other 14-year-old after managing an impossible crisis for 36 hours. "Yeah," he sighed. "I guess I did tell Brendan that I was going to kill myself, but I don't know if I really wanted to or not. I don't think I did but I felt so bad about what I said about him. It, you know, got real weird around 3 [AM]. I was like screaming in my posts that I'm *not* gay." Then he looked ashamed. "Yeah, well, what I really wrote was that I was not 'some f--king fag bitch like Brendan.' When I read my post I felt sick, 'cause Brendan is a friend—probably my *best* friend."

He shook his head in self-disgust. "He's the *only* one who stuck with me through all this. And he's, you know, gay. So when I saw what I typed, knowing he was reading it, that's when I just wanted to die. You can't take it back once you hit *send*. What's really crazy is that I don't care about anybody being gay. So why would I say stuff like that? And how do you prove you're *not* gay?"

Dylan had been on a screen for 11 hours straight through the night, reading in horror and responding in panic as a social network site accumulated dozens of denigrating and hateful postings about him to include even *accusations that he had raped small children.* I could explain Dylan's exhaustion-induced hate rant to him. I couldn't explain how you prove on the Internet that you are not gay or why you should ever have to prove your sexual orientation, whatever it might be—and to have to do that with most every person in the world who knows you.

—From the author's personal journal

■ **Cyberbullying.** Cyberbullying has evolved along with screens. There are now entire websites devoted to nothing but saying hateful things about your kid. Remember that jerk who mocked you in front of three kids, and how painful that was? Now his present-day representative can anonymously push a button and drag your child down in front of everyone who knows of her in any way. And he never even has to see the pain in her eyes. Better brutality brought to you by terrific technology.

■ **Addiction.** I'm referring here to addiction to those screens. Rhianna's phone-throwing words (cited previously) suggested one aspect of addiction, as in being compelled to do something you know is bad for you. Researchers found that some teens actually experience withdrawal symptoms when they cannot access their screens, even when they want to quit. Is there a shoulder patch for that?

■ **Focus issues.** "Attention all ninth graders: Anyone who thinks he does *not* have ADHD, please raise your hands. OK. You three report to the nurse for drug testing since, well, there's just no way." That joke reflects the unfunny fact that increasingly, research points to those ubiquitous screens as being a large contributor to the "everybody's got ADHD" epidemic.

■ **Desensitization/aggression.** The research is no longer split about whether viewing screen violence (including games and violent porn) creates violent teens. Most experts, though not all, have concluded that there is in fact a connection between what kids play on a screen and what they do in the world. And virtually everyone agrees that screen violence causes teens to not react properly to real violence when it occurs in real life. Just now, as I was reviewing the tech-based desensitization research for this book, a story broke about an 18-year-old girl who *live-streamed* the violent rape of her 17-year-old friend, giggling as the horror unfolded in front of both her and her enthusiastic live screen audience, who were increasingly "liking" her "work" as the brutal rape progressed. The stunned prosecutor soberly quoted the videographer's explanation about why she didn't call the cops as her friend sobbed and begged for help: "She said she 'got caught up in the likes.'"

■ **Sexual dysfunction.** An ever-increasing number of young males are reporting erectile dysfunction when engaging in normal sex (I doubt you ever recall that being an issue) unless aggressive/violent pornography or similar screen action is involved. Recently, there has also been a spike in young females who can enjoy sex only if aggression/violence is part of it. This is startling new ground for sex researchers who thought most females were innately wired against porn or violent sex. While the experts are cautioning that there are too few studies to make a definite causal link, most admit it is hard to dismiss the vivid correlation between these numbers and the unprecedented levels of violent porn viewed by our kids.

■ **Sleep disturbance.** Those cool screens that we give to teens act like scary energy drinks, revving up their brains and keeping them awake for at least an hour after they hit the off switch (assuming they ever do). So could losing a few hours of sleep mean much? Read on about teen wellness and see how.

Wellness: Terrorists Don't Need the Nukes . . .

. . . because our kids are killing themselves. Your teenager's generation is on track to become the first in modern history that might not outlive their parents. Ironically, as science offers us amazing insights into the importance of being well, our kids are setting records as being the least well, both when compared with teens from other countries and with their predecessors from this one (us parents). In what ways, you ask?

■ **Sleep, as in too little of.** Your teen needs nine hours of sleep every night. If she's lucky, she gets six, which is roughly the equivalent of you as an adult getting four. Many live on less (if you can call that living), a thing I call the 27/7 syndrome, where they live as if they have 27 hours in their 24-hour day. Guess which part gets shorted? But if losing a few hours of sleep seems like no big deal, let's cut your nightly sleep by about a third (like your kid probably does) and check you out in a few months. Might you be a little ADHD, depressed, and/or anxious? Maybe a little over-reactive and snappy, especially in the morning? How would your job be going? Could you even get so exhausted that not living begins to look OK? How resilient would you be? And you have adult levels of self-control and discipline.

Your answers to those questions should help you understand that some frighteningly large percentage of what we diagnose, therapize, and powerfully medicate as adolescent mental illness is actually *sleep deprivation*. Adolescence has always been an age where nature advances teen "sleep clocks" further into the night, but their new culture has piled on to this problem. The sleep thieves include their tech, their over-scheduled lives, and the bizarre fact that we send them to school way too early in the morning. (When I become king of the world, edict number one will be that your kid gets nine hours of sleep *every* night. Good thing I'll be king because I'll likely be out of work.)

■ **Weight, as in too much of.** Another "us versus them" statistic shows that over the past five decades, the rates of teen obesity (defined as a Body Mass Index of 29) have *quintupled* to where roughly 14 percent of our teens now qualify for this life-threatening disorder. Mind you, that's just the morbidly obese number. Excessive weight (BMI 25–29) claims about a third of our kids. These, again, are epidemic numbers. You can Google the physical health impacts of those BMIs and see why this generation may be the first to not outlive their parents. Their excess weight and their resilience-crushing mental illnesses (depression and anxiety) often go hand-in-hand. Health experts tell me the culprit is (again) the teen culture, including the tech (exercise-killing TV, gaming, Web surfing, and so on) and exposure to carpet-bombing levels of powerful ads that push crippling foods that addict our children to carbs and sugar. They also often cause exquisite pain that you never see.

> Jamal was done pretending, at least for today. In sessions, he often made jokes about his excessive girth. He laughed his "Fat Albert" laugh, saying that he loved being as he was and how everyone laughed at the way he made fat jokes about himself.
>
> But when I probed that issue today, his eyes suddenly filled with tears. His self-jokes, he said, "are just bullsh-t, man. I do that to myself before they do it to me. It feels better to dis myself than have the other kids disrespect me. That's what I thought. Then today, we're walking down the [street] and we pass crackheads and dealers and gangsters and whores, and you know who [the other kids] get on? *Me!* Like I'm this terrible person 'cause I eat too much. And you know what I did? *I joined in with their jokes*, laughin' and playin' and inside I'm like screaming and crying, and I want to smash their faces. Don't take this wrong, but I felt like, like I was laughing with Nazi dudes telling nigger jokes or something, like I'm not worth taking a stand for."
>
> He paused and then used his "Fat Albert" voice: *"Hey, hey, hey! That's me! The happy fat black kid. The one who wants to kill himself!"*

■ **Weight, as in too little of.** Ironically, the numbers of kids *restricting* their food have also increased every decade since 1950. There are many fewer kids starving themselves to death versus eating themselves to death, but this bizarre polarization of eating pathology has worsened on both ends of the spectrum. Researchers point to screen images as a prime factor (among others) telling the self-starving kids that there is no such thing as thin enough. How was your weight back in the day? You likely recall few kids who were severely over- or underweight, but look at a large group of your teen's peers and you'll see what's going on. But can these screen images really affect your child all that much?

Cultural Prompts: Advertising Pays . . .

. . . especially when you're selling crazy. Just ask the fast food pushers—sorry, I meant the fast food execs. If you think they spend most of their budgets on making delicious food, their advertising departments can set you straight about what really sells the dangerous stuff: screen images and song lyrics. The teen brain is particularly vulnerable to programming through the visual and auditory bombardment that today's tech provides. That barrage of cultural prompts, those sights and sounds conveyed to your child in pixels and earbuds, contain powerful suggestions to think and do things that can be very bad for him.

They also work great selling other types of insanity besides the food and porn craziness. They do even better with drugs and sex.

Drugs: The Ones You're Most Likely to Battle

Reefer Madness: Take out your marijuana information eraser again. You're going to have to change what you think you know.

Your first youthful entry into your knowledge base about

marijuana, when you were about age 7, likely came from weed wackos preaching that it would kill you. You rewrote that when you were 13, when the weed warriors convinced you pot was harmless. Your third writing may have come courtesy of today's marijuana moguls, who have carefully studied the old cigarette barons' marketing methods and persuaded the majority of today's teens that pot is not only harmless for them (that's false) but is less immediately lethal than booze (that's true). And those moguls may have convinced you that marijuana should be legalized for the tax benefits. Billions could be added to our government coffers. So what could be bad with that? For your kid, a lot. Because just as with booze, to a teen brain, decriminalization/legalization means the stuff is harmless (and that's definitely not true).

First, know that today's weed should be renamed since the bud you just found in your daughter's backpack (which she was "holding for my friend") is likely 300 to 900 percent more potent than what you may have sampled in your day. (Try taking 6 to 18 laxatives instead of the recommended dose of 2 and you'll get the point.)

Second, the powerful cultural prompts—which include the "weed is harmless" research, celebrity endorsements, song lyrics, social media postings, and parents who not only do weed but allow their kids to partake as well—are all based mostly upon experience with that old puny drug, not the new powerful one.

Third, lots of new science is showing that teen brains undergo specific brain wiring changes and *possible permanent brain damage* from marijuana (for example, a potentially nonreversible eight point drop in IQ). As you'll see shortly, adolescent brains are vastly different from adult brains, with unique responses and vulnerabilities. MRIs show that weed attacks the teen brain wiring in the areas that have to do with learning, specifically in brain regions devoted to problem solving and memory.

While experts argue back and forth about the risks of marijuana for adults, the bottom line is that I know of no legitimate researcher who says it's OK for teens to do weed. Not one. Don't be "cool" with this, even when your kid hits you with the line the weed barons pitch: "Yes or no: Would you rather I drank alcohol?" Your answer, of course, should be: "Yes or no: Do you still torture puppies? Nice try, son, but my answer is that I expect you to not torture puppies, drink alcohol, or smoke weed." (In Part III, we'll fully arm you for those discussions.)

Booze Blindness: Many parents do prefer their teens to drink rather than smoke marijuana since alcohol is largely our adult drug of choice. But alcohol is a terrible drug for teens, arguably worse than weed. When cops are racing to adolescent car crashes, fistfights, and sexual assaults, they're usually unpacking their breathalyzers since they know they'll likely find empties at the scenes.

Weed and booze can both lead to three other potential teen tragedies. The first is addiction, either to these drugs or the next ones. Both can serve as gateways in that they can stop providing the biochemical payoff of initial use and thus make the next drug look really good (or absolutely necessary). In my years of work with addictions, I never met an adult heroin user whose first drug was heroin (although that can happen). Many adults start down the heroin trail with a valid prescription for painkillers, but the vast majority report doing weed and/or booze as teens and then slowly graduating upward. It's a tad unusual for kids to go from stone sobriety to sticking needles in their arms, about as unusual as seeing Big Foot at the opera. But kids who start using alcohol or weed weekly at age 14 have a *500* percent increased risk of full-blown addiction than those who wait until adulthood to use.

There is research that suggests that perhaps 80 to 90 percent of teens who do marijuana or alcohol regularly never graduate to more dangerous ones. If that makes you less worried about your teen using weed or booze, I would ask you this question: If you saw a cool roller coaster that had a small sign reading "Warning. Every 10th teen on this ride loses their life," would you allow your child to climb aboard? Addiction is an absolute horror of a disease that essentially takes the hearts and souls of its surviving victims, often for decades, so that they are living a life that many see as worse than death. Any parents who are "cool" with their kids smoking or drinking are also being cool with tossing dice with the devil for the lives of their teens.

The second tragedy that these drugs offer is their apparent unique ability to "cure" the stress, anxiety, and depression sweeping across this generation of teens (as we discussed in Chapter 1). The devil guarantees his products. Those pains do magically go away, at least for about an hour or so. And that hour can feel like flat-out heaven to an overstressed teenager. But as the drugs wear off, they actually *increase* depression, anxiety, stress, and even suicidal thinking in those already struggling adolescent brains, making the teens feel even worse for a lot longer than an hour. And that makes using again look very good, which increases the bad feelings, which makes using again look very good . . . And that downward spiraling effect can create addiction just as a strong, rotating thunderstorm can create a killer tornado.

The third drug tragedy cuts to the point of this book. You could not chemically tailor a better toxin for teen resilience than drug use for two reasons. First, regular use essentially freezes the social/emotional levels of young teens through the very years when they're supposed to do their greatest growth. (Does "45 going on 15" sound familiar when thinking of your "pothead/ shothead" friend?) Second, since the drugs do anesthetize the worry, the worrier never gets stronger because she doesn't go through the critical resilience-building exercise called standing up to the stress and coping. Agonizing over your history paper? Paralyzed about the pretty girl perhaps rejecting you when you ask for a date? Baffled about how to handle that bully? Well, just light up or run some shots and all of that pain miraculously goes away. Of course, so does that critical resilience-building, stress-reducing therapy known as *coping with the stressor*. This is the core of the antimotivational side effect of all drugs, not just weed. That term paper is never completed, the pretty girl is never called and the bully is never confronted. Ask Max:

> "My parents, they're like, 'You don't give a shit about nothin'! You're supposed to graduate next year, you're flunking every-thing, and all you care about is hanging with your friends and gaming.' They're like, 'Don't you ever worry?'" Max shook his muddled head, trying to shake the weed fog out of his brain, his eyes still glassy from getting high before our session. "Of course I worry. Damn, man. I'm like scared sh-tless about my life. I can't stand thinking 'bout it. Don't they know that's why I get high all the time?"

Sex: What's Good for the Goose May Not Be So Good for the Gander (and Maybe Not So Good for That Goose Either)

It's hard to find cultural prompts in the teen world that don't involve sex. Take an hour and look and listen to what they see and hear in that hour and you will be stunned. Starting with their first access to tech, our kids are pretty much required to become sexual creatures long before they're ready to handle those complex pressures, which can crush their resilience. Becoming sexual does not necessarily mean having sex but rather having to form a code of sexual conduct, at incredibly early ages—codes that are complex and difficult even for us adults.

Tony looked very serious, his brow furrowed in moral pain, as he thought about the implications of having had sex with his girlfriend: "Now that we've done it, everything changed. Other guys are, like, 'Just move on to the next one' like it's a game about who can get the most girls." He shook his head. "They think I'm gay or something 'cause I want to be loyal to her, even though she says it's all cool, that I don't have to be loyal. But I think she's lying. I think she's in love with me. I think she'd be hurt real bad if I got with someone else. She went to the hospital last year for cutting herself. Now that we've done it, I feel like I owe her, you know, like I'm supposed to take care of her so she doesn't get depressed again."

He picked furiously at his hands. "The really, really bad part is that, since we did it, I'm like not into her as much as I was before. But she's way more into me than before." He looked up at me with pained eyes as a torrent of questions poured out. "That's horrible, right, that I'd not want to be with her as much now, when she is more into me? And is this all because we had sex? What the hell do I do? Stay with her forever so she doesn't get depressed again? Do I owe her that? Can I even do that? And if I stay with her and pretend I like her, is that fair to her?" He sighed a huge sigh, pulled his hood over his head, and slumped back into the couch. Tony was 13 years old.

Many adults are surprised to hear that young males have sexual consciences. The only ones more surprised are the boys themselves, who've been taught by their culture that sex is only a fun pastime and that girls are there only to be used and often abused. Researchers have found that powerful cultural prompts can effectively teach boys that girls are all like those women they see in porn, that all they are about is having sex with males who obviously don't care about them. Many boys just accept those views from the cultural prompts, sometimes for decades of lonely sexual immaturity (and brutality). The higher-character boys learn painfully that it's just not that way for most girls, but only after the boys have already "committed" at an age when their brains are incapable of handling such pressures and conflicts (as you'll see in Chapter 3). Yet another recipe for stress, anxiety, and depression.

Girls, of course, still suffer the most. The cultural prompts force them into the sexual arena at far too early ages, and they quickly learn the game is rigged—the same as it ever was.

For five prior sessions, 14-year-old Chloe had promised to tell me "what was really going on" but could never get the words out. "I have to feel I can trust you, and I just can't yet. Trust is hard for me." In our sixth session, she decided to gamble. "Like forever, I got teased for being a virgin. My school [actually, not the school but the kids who go there] has a [social media] page for loser prude girls who haven't had sex, and I was on the list. I got teased all the time. Two months ago, I had sex with some boy at a party. My friends were all pushing me to do it, to stop being a prude. Now, I found out I'm on a slut list." She knew what I was going to ask. "The boys, I don't think there really are lists for the boys like that. There is one, but it makes the boys who have lots of sex look cool." She could not have looked much sadder.

You can loosen your white-knuckled grip on the edges of this book since that about wraps up our scary whirlwind tour of your kid's world. In Part III, we'll give you the tools you need not only to get your teen through all of those challenges but to actually build the magic of resilience—that psychological body armor that will protect him in all the other fights to come.

By the way, if you think that these threats can be worsened by socioeconomic class, you're right. But if you think that having some money completely protects teens and that being poor completely condemns them, you're wrong. Many of these threats get worse as the money gets better. Interestingly, poverty *can often be a promoter of resilience* when poor parents use the strategies and tactics you'll be learning shortly.

Whether rich, poor, or somewhere in between, all of those threats to your kid are made much worse by the sheer timing. They hit just when your kid is, neurologically speaking, getting crazy. Time to turn the page and take a look at the stress-promoting, resilience-attacking, bubbling mass of carbon known as the adolescent brain. Better get a cup of coffee first. Make it strong.

THREE

Teen Brains

Their Minds Are Not All Right
(But That's How It Should Be)

Kate had sad circles under her eyes and shellshock in them. I was guessing this was her first tour in parenting a 13-year-old. "Nicole has been pretty much the perfect daughter all her life," she began. "We had about zero trouble with her. Everything was so easy and positive—and *fun*. School, friends, our relationship, it just all seemed to flow. We never gave it a second thought. Ron and I, when we saw or heard about teens acting crazy, we used to get smug, saying what bad parents they must have to allow them to act like that. One time we were in a restaurant and this teenage girl was screaming and cursing at her mom, yelling something about wanting her mother to let her order whatever 'f--king food' she wanted. I remember judging that mom for allowing her daughter to act like that. We had no idea how good we had it." She sighed heavily.

"Over the past month with Nicole, we've had, I don't know, three explosions like that. And one much worse. Last Tuesday, I politely reminded her to please empty the dishwasher and she went *insane*, out of the blue. Almost foaming at the mouth. When she called me a 'f--king bitch,' she was so close to my face that I could smell her cherry lip gloss, which, by the way, I really, really hate. I just lost it. I, I . . . I slapped her face." Kate looked terribly ashamed. "I know that's so wrong. We've never, ever hit her, not even a whack on the butt when she was small. We never had to! We were so sure we were great parents. Anyway, Nicole just stared at me for a second and then attacked me like a wild animal, punching and scratching me. I tried to hold her as best as I could and Ron ran in and bear-hugged her and put her in her room.

"I was still sobbing downstairs when suddenly blue and red flashing lights filled the house and someone pounded on the door. Nicole had called 911 to say she was barricaded in her room because her father was trying to kill her. This gets worse. One officer ordered Ron to put his hands behind his back. Ron wasn't listening, he was trying to explain what had happened and he took a step toward the cop and raised his hands in exasperation. The officer wrestled him to the floor and handcuffed him." Kate looked into my eyes, hoping for some understanding. "He's an *accountant*, for God's sake! He's the sweetest, nicest guy you can imagine! We are not the kind of people who would ever hurt our child." Kate took a deep breath and exhaled slowly. "Or so I thought. It's as if we're suddenly living in some horrible nightmare and we can't wake up. Doctor, do you think Nicole is just being a teenager or is she crazy?"

"Yes," I answered.

That answer works well. If Dr. Frankenstein had set out to build a creature with poor resilience (one prone to stress, depression, and anxiety), he would have told Igor to steal a 13-year-old's brain. While adolescent brain growth is the most sophisticated stage in human development, it occurs completely backward, proving that Mother Nature has a great sense of humor. We know this because she wires in impulsivity, risk-taking, and powerful passions first, and then tacks on the wisdom of judgment and maturity several years later, almost as an afterthought, usually just in time to keep parents from running off to Mexico and teens from getting arrested as young adults.

This sardonic wiring evens out eventually, so much of the strategy of parenting a struggling teen is simply playing for time as that neurological maturation occurs. As one battle-weary parent defined his last-stand goal, "Alive at 25!" But left untreated by smart parenting, the anti-resilience programming can get set in those circuits and can last forever (particularly given the teen culture you just toured in Chapter 2). As one example, short-term, normal adolescent tendencies toward self-centered, immediate gratification (think sex and drugs) can become lifelong, hard wired, resilience-killing personality traits if not skillfully addressed by parents. The long and complex neurological explanations of these processes are thoroughly explained in the excellent books listed in the Appendix, but I will save you a lot of time with this Q&A quickie course. This will give you all you really need to know to understand and embrace the strategies and tactics found in Parts II and III.

What Is Happening to My Teenage Child?

What you are witnessing is the true child development miracle, a process much more impressive than his learning to move around or talk. After all, puppies and dolphins can move and make sounds. But just as you begin to think you're a parenting genius, nature decides "enough of this sweet little kid routine" and launches your child on the fantastic neurological adventure toward maturity. Adulthood is a time when she will be able to think very deeply, develop life passions and values, and find meaning and purpose for her existence. She will likely raise children of her own and will probably be able to feed herself as well as provide for those children. I'm not making this up! But note I said this would be an "adventure," not a journey. Journeys are typically calmer, more predictable travels where you can see the end and all you have to do is get there safely. Adventures are very different. Ask any rabbi.

Aaron was a great dad. He planned out everything for his kids. Every detail was always covered. He knew that if he worked so hard and organized so well, he would never have the teen issues he saw other parents having. His daughter was perfect! "Then 13 hit like a tsunami," he said. "Pretty much with her Bat Mitzvah [Jewish coming of age ceremony], she went nuts! Said I couldn't tell her what to do or where to go anymore. When I told her she couldn't go out last night at 11:30, she said, 'Really!? Watch.' And she left!

"Today I met with my rabbi, I was so upset. He listened and kind of smiled sadly and said some things I remember word-for-word, they upset me so much. He said, 'Aaron, this time coming with your child, this is not a business you can organize with your spreadsheets. This time, this chapter, will be an *adventure*. Parts will be wonderful; parts will be awful. Parts will be terrifying, and parts will be joyful. There is no way of knowing how it will all turn out. So it is with adventures. That's what makes life so interesting, no? So stop making yourself crazy thinking you can control this. Aaron,' he said, 'remember, *Mann traoch, Gott Lauch*.' That's Yiddish for 'Man plans, God laughs.'"

Having parented two teenagers, I've recited that phrase only about a million times. There is so much wisdom in those four words. They help us to understand that not only is it pointless to attempt to fully control this process, but we can make everyone even crazier when we try. Your child is going to become whomever he is going to become, and much of that we cannot and *should not control*. Read on to find out why.

What Are the Side Effects of This Bass-Ackward Brain Wiring?

You've probably begun your own list of effects seen in early adolescence, but if you consult the packaging that came with your kid, it suggests you expect the following to varying degrees. Note that there are many side effects, but these are some of the most noticeable to parents. The descriptive notes are quotes from my case files.

- **Impulsivity** (Parent: "*What—did—you—just—call—me?*")
- **Poor judgment** (Parent: "You really, truly thought Mom's Subaru could ford that creek?")

- **Mood variability** (Parent: "You want to die from loneliness? Literally 10 minutes ago you were queen of the universe!")
- **Explosiveness** (Parent: "OK. Then it was your two-year-old brother who kicked through your bedroom door?")
- **Risk-taking** (Teen: "Mom, I *know* there are some risks in smoking weed at 14. But a man's gotta do what he's gotta do.")
- **Extreme reactivity to occurrences** (Teen: "You don't know what it's like to be in love! I can't eat or sleep or go to school or practice or anything! She's all I can think about!")
- **Selective memory** (Parent: "So you can recite every word of 10,000 rap songs and you can't remember to take the laundry upstairs? You know, the laundry? That stuff in the huge basket you jump over 10 times a day?")

You may have spelled that last side effect, deleting the "s" to turn "selective" into "elective" memory, as in choosing to forget. And of course, many of the "symptoms" listed here can also just be snarky choices, not the result of deficient wiring. But the neurological fact is that these are all behaviors found to be linked to immature adolescent brain wiring resulting primarily from a lack of good connections between different brain regions. For example, when you were driving home yesterday and that road rage jerk cut you off, the back of your brain (the emotional center) fired up with neurologic fury and physical energy, spewing out a bunch of action directives such as blasting your horn, tailgating, throwing fingers, or (if you're male) passing him at 100 mph and then stomping on your brakes. Those impulses were cc'd over high-speed wires to the front of your brain, which sees things a tad differently. The front brain (the logical or executive function center) reviewed those impulses and commented, "Well, he is a jerk but he might be drunk, could have a gun, and definitely is crazy. Are we willing to die over 10 feet of asphalt?" Your front brain hopefully overruled your rear brain and you backed off, feeling slightly pissed off (or mightily if you're male) but nevertheless knowing you've done the smart/logical thing. All of that happened in a nanosecond and you might recall none of it.

In any similarly exciting or provocative situation (think anger, sex, or drugs), your young teenager gets a monstrously higher dose of those emotional back-brain suggestions but does not have the wires sufficiently in place to quickly run those impulses to the logical front brain for review. In addition, even if the wires were connected, the teenage front brain is still undersized. Picture a 600-horsepower Corvette with lousy brakes and you get the idea. Speaking of cars and brakes and front and back brains . . .

Denny Doyle acted like the 40-year-old of our crowd of 16-year-olds. He was smart, terribly serious, got great grades, worked very hard on everything, and was always helping us not be crazy by sternly talking us out of doing stupid things. He saved me from myself on numerous occasions and always lectured me to work harder in school like he did. Naturally I hated him. I also hated his car. It was a very sensible old pile of crap which looked like a bulbous aquarium on wheels. None of us wanted to be seen in it.

One afternoon I had the guys in my car following him driving alone on our way to play basketball. He always drove so safely that it made me insane. He had a rule about never pulling into traffic until he could see absolutely no cars coming in either direction. As we sat behind him waiting for what seemed like hours for him to pull onto a busy highway, I lost it. I started blowing my horn. Short beeps at first, and gradually with increasing duration. Denny was angry, turning around and yelling at me from inside his huge white "aquarium." With the road noise we could hear nothing, so this all looked very funny, kind of like a cartoon. The guys all started laughing and egging me on. Never one to pass up a good joke, I then softly bumped Denny's car with my own. Seeing Denny's head bob from the impact was hilarious, becoming even funnier when his calm, serious, always-in-control face turned red with rage as he turned, flailed his arms and screamed unheard epithets back toward me. Naturally I continued the bumping as the laughter in my car grew and grew. Then I decided to go for the gold. I began to very slowly push his car inches toward the intersection. He was now desperately clinging to his steering wheel, stomping on his brakes as hard as he could and scream-ing over his shoulder at me. No one had ever seen him out of control before. The only screams I could hear were those of my companions who were laughing so hysterically hard that they couldn't breathe.

—From the author's personal journal

Amazingly, no bulbous car or boring kid was damaged that day, a clear point of evidence suggesting that maybe there is a God. Denny, of course, thereafter stayed far away from me, giving me the same stunned looks that you likely give your teen when he does something hurtful, crazy or dangerous. Neither this author at sixteen nor your kid could offer any reasonable explanation of such behavior. But now, perhaps you can at least understand, and more importantly, even empathize with his neurological predicament when he says to you what I said to Denny. When he asked/screamed, "What the hell were you thinking?" I could only offer the truth: "I don't know. It was crazy. Sorry. I guess I wasn't thinking. It just seemed so funny at the time, you know? Um, I guess not."

When Does this Loveliness Begin?

The adventure departure line typically begins when your kid hits double digits at ages 12 to 14, with girls forging ahead roughly 18 months before boys. BTW, ladies, does that fact set off any memory bells? Recall the kids in your sixth grade classroom as the teacher desperately tried to teach. What were the girls mostly doing? Listening, taking notes, and answering questions. And what were the boys into? Launching spitballs, cursing, making rude noises, spitting, and laying their comatose, drooling heads on their desks. Can you recall having the scary thought that one day you'd have to pick a mate out of that genetic (cess)pool?

Now try to remember your solution to that depressing problem. Is that about when you started hanging outside the eighth grade classroom (which worked out OK because most of the girls in there had little interest in their own male peers)? Try to remember that when you hear yourself channeling your mother as you yell, *"For God's sake, why can't you just once date a boy your own age?"*

When Does the Wiring Get Fixed?

Every time I prep to write a parenting book, someone moves that aging-out-of-adolescence finish line. For example, 25 years ago, we said 18; 10 years ago, we said 25. Now we see some fine-tuning occurring into the early 30s. OMG indeed! The worst of the deficits are usually fixed by 18. But note, that's *just the wiring*. What we *program* into that wiring is a whole other discussion that we'll have in Parts II and III.

Please Tell Me Something Positive

Sure. When it's not terrifying or enraging, this process is absolutely breathtaking. As those brain regions connect, you see your child making astounding leaps in all sorts of capabilities, including learning, judgment, thinking, coordination (in music and sports), compassion, empathy, motivation, and emotional control. And also in a thing called resilience, which we'll discuss in Part II.

Why Would Mother Nature Do This to Me?

As with the Mafia, it's not personal, just business. Mother Nature has a method to her madness. This sometimes frightening, often maddening, mostly chaotic process seems to be incredibly effective in helping your kid to accomplish her primary task of adolescence: *to figure out who the heck she is*. As much as Aaron (the father quoted previously) would love to believe that we can smoothly "organize" our kids into adulthood, it just doesn't work that way. Think about yourself for a moment.

Where did you learn your most defining qualities and values? From calm, quiet successes based on unquestioning acceptance of all those lectures from your parents, or from painful failures where you perhaps radically tested what you had been taught, only then to solidify a value, saying something like, "That was freaking awful. I'll never do that again. That is not who I am or who I wish to be."

Why Did Our Son Go Through This with Hardly a Whimper, While with Our Daughter It's World War III?

When I'm asked that question, I usually respond that according to parent karma, you were sent the apocalyptic daughter as payback for the easy son. Even if that theory is one day proved to be untrue, the fact is that with all things human, there is unending complexity and variability. One hundred individuating factors— including innate personality characteristics (e.g., adaptive or oppositional), specific capabilities (e.g., intellectual, social, emotional), and early childhood experiences (e.g., trauma, family stresses)—all play roles in mediating that teen experience. Sly Stone, that famous child development expert, depicted it perfectly in "Family Affair" when he wrote:

> *"One child grows up to be*
> *Somebody that just loves to learn*
> *And another child grows up to be*
> *Somebody you'd just love to burn."*

But the wiring/maturation process is essentially the same for each teen whether it shows or not. That is why that perfect son can go from being someone who "loves to learn" to someone you'd "love to burn" in a New York minute. The shiny veneers on those perfect teenagers are about 1/8-inch thick and can shatter without warning under excessive stress.

In Parts II and III, we'll teach you how to build and thicken those protective veneers through resilience parenting. First, though, we need to give you a wonderful way to view brains that might not only explain what goes on inside teenage heads but inside yours as well. You need to know this so you can help your kid better manage her emotional brain as well as stay calm yourself when she seems not the least bit interested in managing her emotions at all. Even better, you will have some great "mental judo" skills to engage with her in ways that won't provoke World War III and might even give you a shot at communicating with her logical brain. Throughout Parts II and III, we will use this brain model for your training. You see, I guessed your next question might be:

How the Heck Can I Work with a Brain Like That?

You can do so by understanding that teenagers are not only a little crazy (as we've discussed) but also suffer from a form of what we used to call multiple personality disorder. But that's OK, because everyone is a little crazy and also has a bit of multiple personality disorder, including us parents. Understanding this can give you a calming insight into your kid's behavior and also help you to control your own. And controlling your own behavior is step one in attempting to influence your kid's. You can see this multiple personality disorder operating in places like donut shops all the time.

Of Egos and Eclairs

Hi, everyone. My name's Mike and I'm an addict. My drug of choice is sour cream donuts. *Powdered* sour cream donuts. I am powerless over them. My wife can eat just one and be fine. Me, once I have one, I eat all I can get my hands on. This morning, as I drove to work after a rough, sleep-deprived night with my teen daughter (she hates me for ruining her life, but I can't recall exactly why this time), I realized I needed a chemical boost. I pulled into the donut shop to get a mild stimulant: "Black, three sugars." As the logical region of brain (we'll call it Part 1 for now) flatly ordered coffee, my emotional brain region (Part 2) went squampers over the amazing sight and smell of, yep, racks of freshly baked sour cream donuts, the powered type. A vicious multiple-personality bar fight broke out in my head.

"*Donuts!!*" yelled Brain Voice 2.

"Bad for us," answered Brain Voice 1.

"*Come on!*" whined Voice 2. "We work hard, we work out, and we eat healthy, boring food. We deserve a couple of donuts! Besides, our daughter was horrible to us last night and you didn't let me punch her in the face like I really, really wanted to. We deserve a little comfort food. Get six, eat one, and take the rest home for the family."

"Nope," said Voice 1. "That trick never works. We always eat all six before we get to the office."

"I swear to God," begged Voice 2, *"this time I know we can do this. We'll just eat one! The donut guy is offering us a free-bie! Please, please, please?!"*

"Nope," Voice 1 said. "I know we'll be sorry later if we take that free donut. The discussion is over." Voice 1 then grabbed control of the vocal cords that Voice 2 was about to hijack and spoke aloud, "Just the coffee, please."

Voice 2 launched into a tantrum: *"I hate you! I hate this! I hate the world! This sucks! We work so hard, our daughter disrespects us, and we can't have a frickin' donut?"*

"Yeah, I know," soothed Voice 1. "You have every right to feel upset. But I also know we'll feel better about this later to-day. I'm good at predicting the future."

"I don't care about the future!" Voice 2 yelled. *"I want donuts— now!"*

Suddenly, a new voice chimed in from another brain region (Part 3): "You know, it's ridiculous that even at this point of your life you are so weak that you still want to pig out on do-nuts. What a loser." I walked out of the donut shop having made the right decision and feeling not only deprived but a loser as well. Am I insane?

_____

A mostly based-upon-fact vignette from the life of the author, offered with apologies to Narcotics Anonymous

Do you ever argue silently with yourself just like you do loudly with your kid? Ever go back and forth inside your head about doing something you know you should do and don't feel like doing? Taxes, laundry, exercise, or dental appointments, per-haps? And do you ever have internal brain battles about wanting to do something you know is a bad idea but promises to feel great in the moment? Maybe with drugs (remember that alcohol is a drug), driving too fast, cheating on your partner, or even worse, buying sour cream donuts, the powdered type? Kind of weirds you out when you think about yourself not really being just one person, right?

Psychologists and philosophers from way back have pondered this multiple personality question and have generated many different explanations that keep returning to one basic premise: that inside our heads, each of us has different sets of brain aspects/regions/circuits that can act as *uniquely different creatures*, often competing for control of the bodies in which they find themselves, and often presenting an endless set of mixed emotions about our ultimate decisions.

The great psychiatrist Sigmund Freud (1856–1939) largely gets the credit for originating a three-part structural way of viewing ourselves. He thought human brains were made up of three components he named the superego, the ego, and the id. Freud believed these components fought periodic battles (conflicts) as we develop through life. He further thought that resolving those fights could be accomplished through psychoanalysis, a therapy that often involves several sessions a week over the course of several years. In the 1960s, one rebellious (some say angry at being peer-rejected) Freudian analyst set out a theory he described as "post-Freudian." It simplified Freud's complex views into what was then ridiculed as a simplistic pop-psychology version.

The guy's name was Eric Berne (1910–1970), and he created functional, easy-to-grasp labels for Freud's superego-ego-id system, using instead the terms *parent* {P}, *adult* {A}, and *child* {C} ego states. He tweaked (Freudians say he savaged) how Freud defined these ego states and offered this as a simple system of understanding human behavior. Many experts have detested the popularity of Berne's simplistic system ever since. The problem for those purists was/is that this simple {P}-{A}-{C} view (called Structural Analysis) worked great in therapy, especially with adolescent clients, even though it had no hard scientific basis.

In the decades after Berne created it, Structural Analysis became a treatment model often secretly employed by therapists. They would only quietly admit to using it late at night after a few beers at the psychology conventions, and only then after scanning the bar for some of their peers who would go crazy upon hearing it. (Yes, psychology and politics do have an amazing amount in common, but that's for another book.) Then a strange thing happened: Some new, cutting-edge, researched-up-the-wazoo, embraced-by-purists therapy models appeared that in many ways supported many of Berne's previously dissed speculations. For example, supporters produced MRIs showing unique sets of brain circuits firing up in conjunction with what Berne labeled adult and child ego state behaviors/thought processes.

These newer therapy models, such as cognitive behavioral therapy (CBT) and dialectical behavioral therapy (DBT), proved wonderfully effective in helping folks get better by first teaching people to distinguish their "rational/logical/thinking" brain in the front of the head from their "emotional/feeling" brain in the back. If that rings a bell for you concerning our chat about teen brain maturation, you've got a good bell. More important, CBT and DBT then teaches clients how to manipulate and manage their thoughts and feelings in ways that fix problems. This stuff really works!

The professional complaining that will ensue from the secret I'm about to share with you will be loud. The brain researchers will say it is a gross oversimplification of complex neurological processes, and the CBT, DBT, and other therapy model advocates will call it a mishmash of several carefully constructed theories, and I agree with all of this. But whether or not future research finds specific {P}-{A}-{C} centers in the brain, the fact is that for many/most of us teen therapists, this simple construct works great as a way for teenagers to visualize, understand, and manage their conflicting "crazy" thoughts and feelings. After I teach this concept to kids for only 45 minutes, I see amazing relief on their faces. It perfectly fits with their internal processes and gives them a simple, easy-to-use paradigm to find their way out of previously enslaving thoughts and feelings. Let me lay it out and you can decide if it makes sense to you.

Aspects of Structural Analysis

The {C} or child ego state operates much like a four-year-old. It is a ball of emotion that is directed by powerful feelings that make up all that exists in a particular moment. While making decisions, the {C} cannot really recall the past or organize it as science to predict the future, and it cannot really even conceptualize the future, let alone care about a future time that does not exist. The {C} is all about immediate experience and gratification, and if that gratification is denied, it can literally feel like the end of the world to that {C} brain. Ironically, Mother Nature gave the {C} brain the "nuclear codes" of extreme behaviors (rage, panic) by linking many physiological processes to the {C} wiring. Eons ago, this made evolutionary sense since going into a rage or fear state helped us survive real threats from saber-toothed tigers and angry mammoths. This is the "fight or flight" response you learned about in bio class, where your body surges with Incredible Hulk strength and energy from adrenaline and such. The problem is that four-year-old brains running 14-year-old bodies can be scary.

The {P} or parent ego state does a bunch of things, but the one you need to know about concerning your teen is self-judgment. When you make an error, do you ever call yourself names? Can you feel shame or guilt for having made an honest mistake? (Just now I did when I realized I had made an organizational error in this writing. Inside my head I heard, "What an idiot! You're not organized again! What the hell are you doing?!" If the error was serious, I would hear, "You'll never get this book done in time! What a loser!") If your teen is painfully honest, they likely will tell of hearing these internal put-down voices much of the time, often so much so that they wish they were no longer alive: "You are so ugly/fat/skinny/stupid/uncool/nerdie/insane/lazy/uncoordinated/cowardly/hopeless you should die." Their list seems endless and that voice seems so very loud and so very correct and unimpeachable. Left unchallenged, that part of the {P} brain can do terrible, lifelong damage like an internal neurological bully.

The {A} brain is our salvation, both individually and as a species. Brain researchers often call this structure the "seat of civilization," and it is indeed a flat-out miracle bequeathed by God or Mother Nature or whomever you blame for your present parental predicament. That {A} brain can recall the past, organize those experiences/observations into science, and then use that not only to predict the future with amazing accuracy but to conceptualize and *care about a time in the future that does not exist*. That is freaking amazing! It is reasonable to claim that the {A} brain is the reason we have survived thus far on this planet. It's also the brain part that helps us to find meaning, passion, and purpose in life. What's more, it can manage the bad parts of the other ego states. As we've already shown, the {A} brain can quell the destructive impulses of the {C}. And it can talk back to the put-down voice of the {P} and argue that we are in fact OK: "Wait a minute. I'm a good person. I just made an honest mistake. You don't know what you're talking about."

Berne's theories are much more complex than what I've presented here, and in the Appendix, I've recommended a few other books to dig deeper if you are so inclined. But the few essentials here give you the basics you need to understand and employ the resilience-building strategies and tactics we'll teach in Parts II and III that are predicated on Structural Analysis.

Some other {P}-{A}-{C} concepts, however, bear mentioning here. First, when we diagram someone in those terms, we like to argue that these ego states should be equally sized circles, meaning that they are all essential and each offers good points as well as bad. For example, the {C} is the likely source of creativity, spontaneity, and humor, things that largely define us as humans and contribute mightily to our survival and happiness. And the {P} can be very useful in regulating behaviors with codes or rules of conduct. It can also sometimes be consoling and nurturing when we need internal reassurance.

We like to conceptualize the {A} as centrally located between the {C} and {P}, monitoring those {C} and {P} processes and jumping in to take control as needed. In case you haven't noticed, your teen has a huge self-critical {P} and a huge impulsive {C}, with a small {A} stuck in the middle often asking, "Why the hell do I hate myself?" and "Why the hell did I just do that?" The age of adolescence is when that {A} brain grows, connects, and begins to take charge *if* we skillfully manage our teen in ways that build the magic of resilience—a task largely about empowering that {A} brain.

So now you know that teenagers' brains have severe challenges (Chapter 3), that their culture inflames those challenges to encourage them to get crazier (Chapter 2), and that consequently they are suffering at historic rates (Chapter 1). "But Dr. B," you point out, "they have us parents to get them through, right?" Well, in fact, we can be part of the problem or part of the solution when you think of resilience parenting. The comics character Pogo, created by Walt Kelly, once paraphrased a famous battle report in a way that too often applies to resilience-focused parenting: "We have met the enemy, and he is *us*." Turn to Chapter 4 and you'll see what I mean.

FOUR

Us

Their Parents
Are Not Doing So Great Either

"Weakness is tiring; strength is exhausting."
From the screenplay *Nicholas Nickleby* (2002)

I understand if you want to skip this chapter. By far the hardest aspect of parenting adolescents in the new millennium is what goes on inside the hearts and minds of parents trying to make journeys (where you can see the end) out of adventures (where you have no idea where you're going). Nicholas Nickleby's quote above would make a great parenting T-shirt. As this chapter will show, it's very tiring to attempt to force our kids to become what we want them to be. It's a lot of well-intended work that, in excess, can damage their resilience. Doing less actually builds their resilience more, but the strength required to try not to control their destiny can be exhausting. This is another example of the maddening vagueness of this whole parenting gig. In the best of times we're never sure if we're really doing the best of things. In the worst of times we're positive that we're doing the worst of things. Plus we're usually surrounded by experts who helpfully confirm our incompetence for us:

"My mother-in-law says it's a mistake coming here for counseling," Diane said. "She tells me she raised five kids without any issues and the problem is that we are 'coddling' Matthew with therapy. Do you think that's true? She says we should just make him stop the weed and start studying, that we should get tough and just throw him the hell out if he gives us crap. When I try to tell her that of course we've tried to do those things, she gives me this look that makes me feel horrible, like I'm stupid, weak, uncaring, or maybe all of the above. I explained that we decided to come to therapy because when we tried the tough approach, Matthew ran away. My husband told him to not come home until he was ready to stop the weed and start doing school. That was very 'get tough'—mostly on me! I didn't sleep for two nights, but we held firm. The third night the police brought Matthew to our door. We were sure he was in trouble. Turned out *we* were. The police told us that since he's 15, if we did not let him back in, they would cite *us* for child endangerment and notify child services. Matthew was grinning at us the whole time like he was silently taunting us and pretty much saying, 'I can grow up to be a worthless human being and there ain't nothin' you can do about it.' The cop saw him sneering at us, shook his head, and said, 'Sorry. I've been through this myself. The system seems rigged. Just get some counseling. Sometimes it can help.'

"Now my husband wants nothing to do with him. He says Matthew will have to figure this out on his own since we have no power over him until he turns 18, when we can legally throw him out." Diane started to cry. "By then, won't it be too late?" She took a deep breath and exhaled like an exhausted runner. "Now hardly anyone talks. My husband, he's just mad all the time. I'm just incredibly sad. And confused."

Why Am I So Sad? (Moms)/ Why Am I So Mad? (Dads)

You're sad and/or mad because your child died when she became a teenager. You're likely feeling stupid about thinking that way since technically she's still alive, so you repress that "dumb" (silly *and* silent) grief. When a son first does drugs, or when a daughter first has sex, or when either has their first profanity-laced rage, parents are often devastated with grief. That loss of innocence can cause parents to feel as if their child died. No exaggeration. Unacknowledged and uncontrolled, that sadness can lead to bad parenting—another factor contributing to the epidemic loss of teen resilience.

In Parenting, 1 Is Bad and 10 Is Bad

Think of parent involvement as a 10-point scale. One grief-based parenting response—seen more often in dads than moms—is withdrawal, which is 1 on the 10-point scale. ("The hell with him. He's on his own. Who cares what he does?") Cutting off your kid can feel satisfying in a macho, payback sort of way for a little while, but it's dangerous. There is a huge risk in withdrawing parenting from a brain-challenged creature in the midst of the most transformative changes of his life, and in the midst of a toxic culture that will rush to fill that vacuum with scary prompts. That recipe can cause exactly the kind of resilience loss that creates the suffering we talked about in Chapter 1. You see, parenting up to adolescence is easy. Anybody can do that. The tumultuous teen years are exactly when the most skilled and disciplined parenting is most needed.

But the 10 on that parenting scale (over-engaging) can be just as bad as withdrawal in ways that parents often employ as a grief reaction. Here are some of these "too much" styles:

Becoming angry and authoritarian (drill sergeant/cop). Most of us at least consider this tempting option. It's a handed-down belief that our teens will be safer if we overwhelm them with punishments, screaming, and even hitting (most parents in America still hit their kids). We think that if we are willing to act crazier than an adolescent, then the 14-year-old will concede and give us our 10-year-old back. But as veteran parents can tell you, most teens are willing to get crazier than we are, and they get weird neurological payoffs from dragging us into that rage swamp. Be careful, for that seductive tactic of anger can work for a bit. But when it finally fails, as it always does, after the explosion it will leave a huge smoking crater in your resilience-building capabilities and your relationship with your teen.

Being over-involved and excessively caretaking (helicoptering/hovering). This is where we decide that the cure for crazy is to become enmeshed and micromanage our daughter's 13-year-old self back into her 10-year-old version. While this style usually doesn't cause an explosion, the results can be equally toxic, but quiet. A surprising number of teens will abdicate control of their life choices back to us for a while. It can relieve them of the short-term anxiety of having to deal with the real world: "Mom, the coach is hurting my feelings by benching me for not practicing. Take care of that for me, would you?" Doing stuff like this might build the parent's resilience. But it definitely kills the kid's.

Being permissive/laissez-faire (needing to be the friend, fearing to be the parent). This is where the teen takes charge by threatening to further emotionally withdraw from the parent if the parent dares to act like one: "If you don't let me go to the beer party, I'll never talk to you again and then you'll never know what's going on in my life. I used to think you were cool like Kerri's parents." This clever tactic hits the parental grief scar by threatening further emotional loss. Some of us try to disguise this as a safety measure: "If I make him upset by saying no to the beer party, then he won't tell me when he's doing really dangerous things." So . . . we should keep our communication lines open to avoid his doing dangerous things by, um, letting him do dangerous things?

In their own way, each of these parenting styles damages resilience growth in teens. So what are good parenting numbers? As with most things human, the resilience parenting magic lies in the middle 4-5-6 range—the styles we refer to as authoritative, a near mystical balance of firmness and nurturing ("iron fist/velvet glove"). Parents can vary a tad in either direction (3 or 7) and still be equally effective as long as they hang in that magical middle range. In Parts II and III, we'll unmask the secrets to that magic and teach you the strategies and tactics you need to do that trick well. But for now, know that we all must process that initial "loss of my sweet child" grief straight up and apart from our parenting to keep it from driving our style.

Handling Our Grief

As you may have noticed, our personal needs for power and control already infect our parenting too much. Grief can take us all over the edge. Even the pros who should know better:

My 14-year-old daughter went missing for hours one day, returning late that evening without explanation, saying only, "We'll talk tomorrow." The next morning while driving her to school, I pressed her repeatedly for that accounting, somehow forgetting all the rules about when not to press teenagers for serious talks. Rule number one is never in the morning. But after all, this was for her own good, right? "I promise we'll talk tonight," she replied to my repeated requests. "You know how stressed I get going to school," she pleaded. "Mornings are awful for me. I don't want to get upset on the way there."

"No," I commanded, "we need to talk *now!*"

"No, *we* don't," she said. "*You* do."

Then someone yelled, *"For God's sake stop acting like a two-year-old!"* I was stunned. The yeller was not me; it was her. The 14-year-old was exactly right. *I* was the two-year-old needing to immediately end this awful sadness of losing my little girl to this body-snatching teenage creature who was taking her over, causing her to think and act autonomously, sometimes in ways that terrified me. My "righteous" anger was really my grief pretending to be parenting.

—From the author's personal journal

So how do you handle this grief? It's all about trying to reframe these scary changes from horrible and threatening to normal and positive. The first step is to try to calm yourself by understanding *there very likely is no emergency here*. It takes a while for the true teen crises to begin to take shape. The odds are huge that you have lots of time to ensure your kid's safety from the things that can truly end his life. Snarly and disrespectful is not the same as unsafe. Yet, even knowing that, it still feels kind of like an emergency, right? And it can hurt especially bad if the teen in question is your first or that "special" one among his sibs, the child you secretly felt was closest with you.

But our kids are *supposed* to do this stuff we hate. Like it or not, this is Mother Nature's way, forcing the rebirth of your child, a second "breaking away" process you cannot and should not want to stop any more than you could or would the first such process. The hard part is that the outcome of this second birthing struggle will not be a sweet, cuddly bundle of joy. These second "labor pains" can initially produce an insulting, scary, and defiant bundle of stress. That's because instead of just breaking away physically, this time they leave us by questioning our values, arguing with our requests, and even defying our rules. Believe it or not, those are signs of a coming miracle even greater than their first birth. For this is the true blossoming of a fully autonomous adult, at whom you will one day stare and say, "OMG! It's a miracle! She can think for herself! He can feed himself!" The bad news is that the second labor will be slightly longer than the first, with the most intense contractions typically lasting from three to four years. Human miracles take lots of time.

A second grief handling trick is to understand that you have much less control over this process than you believe. Thinking you can forge the adult you want out of the teen in front of you is much like thinking you could force your baby to have curly hair or green eyes. Most of us labor (pun intended) under the delusion that if we do everything right, we can create those perfect 18-year-olds on the covers of the Marine Corps and Harvard brochures. Then we feel like grief-stricken failures when that trick doesn't work. It actually never works, even when it appears to. The reality is that *we take far too much credit when our teens succeed, and far too much blame when they fail.* Unfortunately, your audience does not think that way and will judge you accordingly as a parent.

A better view is to think of your young teen as an unidentified seedling gifted to you by God, nature, or whoever caused your present predicament as the parent of a teen. You can love, nurture, protect, shape, prune it a bit, and surround it with all the positive things you can, but mostly it will grow up to be whatever it will be. Doing too much to make it what you want might stunt its growth and damage its resilience. It is far wiser to help it to be what was intended and sit back and enjoy the blossoming. The good news is that your seemingly sudden loss of immediate and total control over your child is a sign of a normal and healthy adolescence. The bad news is you can't write the outcome of your teen's life as you'd wish. Did anyone mention this would be an adventure, not a journey?

Ironically, the third grief trick is to know you *do* have lots of parental power, but not in the short-term control form you had hoped. Your power is quiet and its profound impact may not show for several years. Yet wisely wielded, it will overwhelm every other dark influence out there competing to shape your kid. In galactic revolutions and parenting, you must "Trust the Force." Here's a letter I received from the mother of a former patient:

Hi, Dr. B. We last met seven years ago today when my 15-year-old Sophie left to go live with her father. [The parents were divorced.] I remember that date like a death anniversary. Back then we were having terrible fights over everything—boys and school, to name two. I remember hating you for saying that perhaps I had to let her go to her dad's to one day get her back rather than risk losing her forever by trying to force her to stay. At first I couldn't stand the thought of losing my little girl. I got better when I realized my little girl wasn't there anymore. Someone very wonderful took her place, although it took a lot of time. Guess what? The old "I-don't-give-a-crap-about-school" D student graduates from college next month—with honors! Sophie and I did reconcile about five years ago and now we are very close. It's just amazing! And wonderful. . .

Something she said should go into your next parenting book as one of the stories you tell. When I told Sophie I was surprised by her great grades in college because she didn't care much about high school, she said, "Mom, just because I didn't do what you said doesn't mean I wasn't listening. I think I had to hear what you said, and then go away and figure things out myself."

Dr. B, she's become the best parts of me in many ways, particularly my values and morals, the things I really care about. She certainly wasn't imitating me back then! She was doing mostly the exact opposite.

That letter from Sophie's mom very well depicts the power of the most formidable weapon in a parent's arsenal to shape their child: "the Force" of modeling. Our kids are much more influenced by *watching who we are* than by *hearing us say what we want them to be.* The "here's what's wrong with you" lectures are also very powerful in a terrible way. They can drive your kid off into their culture to seek out new models of how to be an adult. Scary thought, no? Remember that your kid's number one resilience-building teen job is to develop her own identity, not to become an extension of yours. Your best bet to influence that process is to silently let her observe you practicing (not preaching) your values and codes and see what they mean to you. Be what you want to see in your teen. Before you try shaping your kid's heart, inventory your own and quickly repair what you need to fix. Remember, she will largely be what she sees: your good, bad, and ugly.

The idea is not to be perfect (any candidates out there?). She will likely learn more from you as an *imperfect* parent than as a perfect one. She can tolerate, forgive, and even relate better to the imperfect parent *as long as* we own our imperfections straight up as opposed to acting as if we are entitled to do things such as scream, yell, and hit.

Hypocrisy and pretense are toxins to your relationship. Conversely, our parental screwups provide wonderful teaching moments. Ever try lecturing your teens about owning their behaviors, wrestling with their imperfections, and striving to be better? After word five, their deflector shields go up and all they hear is "Wah, wah, wah . . ." But if you go to them and apologize for *your* failure (such as screaming), their eyes and ears are wide open since you are criticizing yourself, not them. And those ears are hearing about owning behaviors, wrestling with imperfections, and striving to be better. Apology is another amazing parenting weapon acting like a Trojan horse, sneaking essential teaching into their brains in a disguise of heartfelt admissions. You will never be larger in the eyes of your child than when you make yourself small with an apology.

The fourth grief trick is to try to recall the real deal of your own adolescence and young adulthood, not the "for public release" version we try to pawn off on our kids about how virtuous and industrious we were. How did you develop your own identity? By neatly incorporating all of the wise lectures you were pounded with? Or was it more a messy sausage-making process of doing a thousand things—some good, a lot bad? Was it a process of thinking about what you had done and felt, of seeing the impacts of your actions upon others, and then running all that through a grinder, often to say, "That was awful. I hate how that made me feel. I intend to never feel like that again. That must not be who I am." Some of us learned our best stuff by acting and feeling crummy. David did:

"Last week I asked a girl out, sort of—well, actually, knowing I only wanted sex. She's a nice girl but not the skinniest or prettiest in the school, if you know what I mean. She doesn't get a lot of dates, maybe no real ones, so she sounded really happy when I asked her to go out to dinner. As the night went on I had this plan about how this would go, and then something really crazy happened. She told me about herself, about how hard life was for her at school, getting put down a lot because she was heavy. She told me about other boys trying to get her to 'do stuff' and how awful that made her feel. She wasn't, like, complaining or anything. She was just telling me that to say how much she appreciated that I asked her out in that, you know, nice way.

"I knew right then that my plan had worked. I knew she was having some feelings for me, she thought I was a nice guy, and I could use that to get what I wanted. Then, like, out of nowhere I started to feel really, really crummy. I was shocked that

I felt really, really crummy. She even asked me if I was OK, 'cause I guess I was looking sick or something. So I never tried anything with her. Who knew? I guess I'm always going to be this loser who doesn't get the girls like my friends do. Dude, it really sucks having a conscience. But, you know, I guess it also feels good doing a good thing. Weird."

So try to be patient with your teen's insulting attitude and bewildering, sometimes crummy behaviors. It's all about learning. Sausage making is not a neat process, but the final product can be wonderful.

Why Am I So Confused?

For two reasons. The first is that parenting teens has always been hard, and much of parenting teens today is the same as it ever was. You're confused because your memory sucks and your parents were nice enough to not tell you the real deal of your own adolescence. We parents often do this revisionist history thing where we edit out much of the crazy stuff we did and thought as teens. Our sanitized version seems so different from what we see our kids doing, and we panic at what seems like their extreme disrespect, defiance, and dangerousness. But we all did our own versions of this breaking away process as part of our own journeys to resilient adulthood, and each generation pushes the same envelope a tad, shocking the hell out of their parents.

Over the past five decades, the most horrific teen-to-parent epithet has morphed from *"You're a jerk!"* to *"You're a god-damned jerk!"* to *"You're a mother-f--king jerk!"* The essential

message has remained the same, expressed in a different dia-
lect. Smart people have been worrying about these shocking
behaviors of teenagers for a very long time. One said: "The
children now love luxury; they have bad manners, contempt for
authority; they show disrespect for elders and love chatter in
place of exercise." That quote is usually attributed to Socrates
whining about teenagers some 2,400 years ago. Similar "what's
the matter with kids today" complaints have been lodged ever
since. I'd bet Socrates's parents said the same about his teen
generation.

The second reason you feel so confused is that much of parenting today's teens *is* new territory, and the old rules don't work.
Prior generations of parents mostly defined their job as simply
controlling their teenagers. This old mission continues to be unquestioningly held by many new millennium parents. When researchers ask parents to define their ultimate goal in parenting
their kids, the most common answer is: "We want them to be
happy as adults." When asked how they intend to get that done,
parents usually respond with goals such as making their kids do
well in school, not do drugs, and not become parents while still
teenagers. When we ask how they intend to make those things
happen, they usually speak of control measures such as rules and
punishments. "Let him just try drugs," one dad forcefully as-
serted as he raised a threatening fist, "and he'll learn from me
that ain't gonna ever happen."

My Irish Catholic father never had much involvement in my
life, acting on his ancient and profound belief that parenting
children was "women's work." I remember the exact words of
the only spoken advice I ever recall receiving from him when I
was 16. As I stumbled bleary-eyed and nauseated to the

kitchen table at 8 AM, his terrifying voice growled low from behind his face-covering newspaper: "Don't ever come home like that again." His words powerfully influenced my beliefs and behaviors about drugs. I believed that I should and always did sleep out after drinking.

—From the author's personal journal

As explained in previous chapters, you are in fact facing novel, more powerful, and more numerous challenges than my old man did. Throughout history, each generation of parents was confronted with some new youth threats, but today these changes come at light speed, compressing profound cultural occurrences into smaller windows of time so that contemporary parents always feel behind the curve, catching up to respond to the new threats to their teens even as unprecedented ones appear on the horizon.

This new reality requires that parents embrace a new mission statement that creates a set of values and skills in their teens that allow them to resiliently and autonomously adapt to the new threats without having to simply rely upon the control abilities of the parents, since that won't float the boat anymore. That old mission typically worked in those old worlds since there was much less craziness readily accessible to teenagers. As the unprecedented numbers of suffering teens prove, this world is different. So we need a new mission for this new war in this new world. Control is no longer enough.

So What Exactly
Is My Parental Mission?

To teach your teens to control themselves. I have some bad news. This book will not give you what you or I secretly want as parents of teens. Most of us go to parenting lectures for the same reason my parenting expert peers and I go to shrink/author get-togethers (now there's a truly frightening reality show). We all hope to corner the latest fad shrink with the latest fad book to snag some amazing technique to control our kids: "Hi. I'm Mike Bradley, the noted author and parenting expert. Love your book! Can I ask you a question, not about my own kid, of course, but about a client. If your daughter was dating this creep . . ."

As parents of teenagers, we all harbor this deep wish to control our kids. Secretly, we believe that if they just did everything we told them—embraced all our values, dressed like us, listened to our music—then everything would be wonderful, right? In one way, perhaps yes, but then they would also be living with us when they're 40. We don't want that. To strike out on their own and to make their own way in this crazy world, our kids need—just as we did—a "fire in the belly," a kind of simmering low-level anger they can convert into the courage and energy needed to break away:

> "I'm sick of my parents! I love them and all, but they make me insane! I'm going to work hard at a job, or go to college, or join the military and get the hell out of here and make my own rules! I can do this better than them!"

Hearing those words should make you rejoice, not mourn, since they likely confirm that you did a good job by doing a bad job of simply controlling them. Instead, you wisely opted to teach them to control themselves. If "teaching to control" versus "control" sounds like only parsing a few words, you are correct. But those few parsed words mean all the difference in the strategies and tactics you will be learning, which are all about using that {P}-{A}-{C} information in Chapter 3.

The unending generational redefinition of "devil's music" nicely defines this difference in mission. Circa 1967, my "hoodlum friends" and I were in my father's basement (as he referred to it), listening to what many parents at that time considered to be "the devil's music." The song wafting up the stairs that afternoon was "The End" by the Doors. If you're unfamiliar with it, dial up the song and listen to Jim Morrison's words right after "Father . . . I want to kill you." Be sure your kids are out of earshot.

My father was decades ahead of his time in worrying about the impact of cultural prompts such as lyrics upon neurologically soft teen brains. Upon hearing Morrison scream the next phrase, the old man decided that a skilled parental intervention was appropriate. He wordlessly marched down the steps with his trademark cheap cigar in hand, snatched the album off the record player (remember albums?), and smashed it on the record player, which turned out to be a very effective parental intervention since the shards flew like shrapnel, causing us all to duck for cover. Towering over us (back then he seemed to be approximately 8′6″ or perhaps 8′8″ tall), he replaced the cigar in his mouth, took a drag, and blew smoke in our wide-eyed faces. Then he placed his hands on his hips, waiting for one of us to be dumb enough to sass him back, which we weren't.

We were all cognizant of the Southwest Philadelphia code, which held that anybody's parent could beat anybody's kid and usually be thanked by the kid's parents. (I still carry a dent in my skull from the Polish lady who overheard me trying out profanity. I thought she didn't understand English. Turns out she knew the important words.) Anyway, the old man then turned and marched back up the stairs, snarling and cursing that the "goddamned kids today have no goddamned respect, they curse all the goddamned time . . ." I resisted the urge to remark upon the irony of generational criticism, and we all escaped unbruised.

Question: Was that control-based parenting tactic effective? Before you rush to judgment about how using fear is a lousy strategy, consider that context of 1967. My friends and I were poor by today's standards. No one went hungry, but few had cars, we each owned one good pair of shoes, the city dump behind my house was our playground, and few of us had any "discretionary income." We had begged, borrowed, and stolen to get that Doors album, contributing every penny available. Look up what an album cost in relative dollars in 1967 and you'll feel our pain. *That was the end of the influence of "The End" over us.* We couldn't afford another album. Even if we could, Joey B's sister's record player (which he had stolen for us) had been another casualty of the old man's intervention. And we couldn't hear the song on the radio because DJs could not play the cut as a result of the decency laws existing back then, saying that you can't play crazy stuff that kids might hear and be affected by. It was years before "The End" could harm us again.

You could argue that my father's action *was* an effective parenting tactic since back then you could largely *control your child's environment.* Today, as you read this book, you might overhear your daughter listening to horrific lyrics. If you grab her device and erase that MP3 track, what will she do? Not only redownload it but get two others that are worse, just to show you. And please spare me the drill about how you spy on all of her texts and music. Your kid is much better at the tech "Spy vs. Spy" (remember *Mad Magazine*?) game than you are.

Using fear-based control in today's world is an impossible mission creating an unwinnable war. As we saw in Chapter 2, the contemporary teen world exponentially increases the power of their culture to shape their behaviors, and decreases their resilience skills to cope with those challenges. Our best option is to use resilience-building, respect-based strategies and tactics intended to fulfill the mission of teaching our kids to control themselves using {P}-{A}-{C}. That afternoon in 1967, my old man very effectively targeted my {C} brain. He scared me a lot and taught me little. In our new parenting war, we must go after our kids'{A} brains, where we might teach them something that might help them on their path to resilience. What's that drill look like?

Circa 2003, my 13-year-old son, Ross, was in my basement with his hoodlum friends listening to his devil's music. After overhearing the hoodlums laughing at some lyrics that would have made Jim Morrison proud, I went down the steps (without a cigar) to intervene. My strategies and tactics were a tad different from those of my father. I did not need to be 8'8" and neither do you.

As I hit our loose top step, the squeaky noise somehow shut down the CD player (remember CDs?). Downstairs I found five teen males all standing in absolute silence doing . . . *nothing*?

"Gentlemen," I announced, "we need to put that CD back on." Answering their panicked exchange of looks, I added, "I'm not going to take your CD. I don't even care who owns it. The price we pay is that we all listen to it together, OK?" More panicked looks got shot around as I cued up the machine. Then we heard an "artist" who taught these young men and me critical facts that my professors skipped over in my "Psychology of Women" courses. I'll spare you the gross details, but one salient point stood out as representing my ignorance of the female psyche, namely that women like to get beaten up. I knew this to be true since that artist said that women feel loved when you beat them, even though they cry and plead that they don't. Interesting point, don't you think: *Men, don't listen to what women say since we know what they want better than they do.* OK.

I switched off the CD and reached for the most powerful weapons in my arsenal: *questions.* "Gentlemen," I started, "do you think women like to get beaten up as that song says?"

One smart-assed kid (SAK) sassed back: "That's a stupid question. It's just a dumb song lyric. Who cares?"

"Well," I calmly responded, "do you think this stuff you guys see and hear in your world can affect behavior, as in maybe make some kids more inclined to do what they see and hear?"

"Naw," SAK sneered. "That's stupid. What kids see or hear can't make them do stuff."

"Really?" I exclaimed. "I'll be right back." Then I got a chart I had made for a class I was teaching showing how screen ads are extremely powerful influencers of teen behavior such as cigarette smoking.

SAK sneered at the chart, saying, "Well, maybe that's true for something dumb like smoking, but nothing would make kids beat up girls."

"Really?" I exclaimed. "I'll be right back." I returned with a second chart showing a powerful correlation between the rise of sexually explicit misogynistic lyrics and a corresponding increase in sexual violence against young women. "Now this is correlation, not causation stuff," I explained. "This doesn't prove that the lyrics caused the violence, just that they both happened at about the same time. But doesn't it worry you, maybe a little bit? I'm sure you guys would never hurt a girl like that but maybe some kid you know who's got an anger problem, maybe that kid sort of gets permission from CDs like yours to do something horrible to a girl, especially if he hears you guys laughing at this stuff like it's funny and cool. Maybe he acts out with your sister or maybe to Kimmy, you know, that girl down the street who seems so nice to everyone. Whaddya think?"

SAK sneered again but this time stared silently at his Nikes. The other guys seemed to be thinking. No one was laughing about sexual violence now. Maybe they were learning.

Ross often absolutely hated whenever I did this kind of thing, especially with his hoodlum friends. He used to call it "messing with my mind" (which would be a great title for a book on parenting teens). This particular time, he jumped up and yelled, *"Why don't you just punch me in the face and get this over with?"*

I went once again for my best weapon. "Gentlemen, what would happen if I beat Ross up for doing this? I'd enrage, embarrass, and humiliate him in front of his friends, pushing him further into the influence of that insane message on that CD, something I consider to be my enemy. The best thing I ever learned in the Army was don't start fights you can't win. Gentlemen, I can't win the war with the crazy world around you. I truly wish I could control what you guys see and hear but I can't. The minute I leave, I know this stuff rains back down on your eyes and ears. Gentlemen, I care instead about *what you think* about what you see and hear in your world. If I can convince just one of you that maybe this stuff is dangerous and needs to be stepped up to, then maybe the next time some kid at school is bragging about 'bitch-slapping' his girlfriend, maybe, just maybe, one of you will find the guts to say, 'Hey, man. That's not cool, and that's not funny. You don't need to talk like that. People do get hurt by words.'

"And so, on that note, I've invited Ross's mother to join us to share from a female perspective about whether or not women like to get beaten up and how they truly feel when they hear lyrics such as those. Believe it or not, some girls will laugh along with that crap because they're afraid to speak up." At this point, SAK had his finger down his throat as if to gag himself. Funny guy.

What exactly was I doing? Acknowledging what I can and cannot do. I cannot control their world or their behavior with anger and control, and neither can you. That mission may have been somewhat doable in our parents' and grandparents' wars, but what worked in Korea will not work in today's fights. New special ops missions, strategies, and tactics are needed. Similarly, you and I can win this current fight with our kids' culture by shaping their beliefs with quiet, respect-based questions that make them think. Change a belief, and you change a person. Change a person, and you change a community. Change a community, and then maybe the world shifts a bit. But it all starts with one person and one belief.

As new millennium parents, we can no longer effectively police our kids' world as your parents may have been able to do with yours. Nor will simple control measures keep them safe or build their resilience. There is no way to keep the insanity away from them. Your enemies arrive through your wire and over your walls. They're likely indoctrinating your teen at the very moment you're reading this book (tell me she's not on a screen, wearing headphones, or both). You must acquire the surgical strike skills involved in teaching teens to *control themselves*—a mission also known as resilience parenting—a process that focuses less on immediate control and more on developing specific skills in both you and your kid so that you can both adapt to whatever new future craziness comes down the line.

We're going to give you a whole bunch of those what-to-do-when suggestions similar to the example above throughout the rest of this book. So if you're ready, take a breath, turn the page, and enter Part II to start your specific skill training in the strategies and tactics of resilience-based parenting. As those parenting experts in the Marine Corps love to shout, "Welcome to Parris Island, Maggots!"

Strategies and Tactics

Now that we've defined your mission, it's time to give you the strategies and tactics you need to pull it off. Before we proceed, I need to share my concern that my use of military metaphor could worry or even offend some parents with its inference of extreme hostility and stress. While I (like Jim in the Preface) have found that at times parenting teens can push us to and beyond our emotional limits, the military metaphor is more based upon the concept of attempting to bring purposeful, productive, and goal-oriented order to chaotic and occasionally dangerous situations, be they military or adolescent. The thankful fact is that the overwhelming majority of uniformed folks never hear a shot fired in anger, and yet their work can still be incredibly challenging and exhausting. Try safely setting up a small city in the middle of a hostile wasteland in a few days and you'll get the idea. These Herculean tasks are pulled off only through meticulously detailed planning, discipline, and practice based upon this organizational concept of a clear mission supported by broad strategies expressed through very specific tactics defining day-to-day actions. Important and risk-laden jobs, such as setting up a fire base in a Middle Eastern desert or raising a teenager in this new world, don't happen casually. This same mission-strategies-tactics model is also well used by religious institutions, charities, corporations, and educators in solving complex and challenging problems. When the stuff hits the fan, planning and training help limit the splatter.

With that pleasant metaphor in mind, you're now ready to begin your specific skill training in learning the strategies of re-silience parenting, which are the stepping stones toward your mission of helping your teens to control themselves. Chapter 6 will give you some specific day-to-day tactics to accomplish these objectives. But first, in Chapter 5, we must define these strategies and see how they are achieved.

Author's note to arrogant readers such as me: If you have picked up my bad habit and skipped the first four chapters of this book to get to the "what-to-do stuff," you will likely have to do as I always do and be forced to go back to read those chapters. This takes more time and works less well than a straight read-through. If you've skipped ahead, you won't fully under-stand the rationale behind the strategies and tactics, and that can lessen the conviction you need to carry out these actions. Amer-ican military officers are trained to explain a mission's rationale to their people since their research proves that understanding the "why" of a situation substantially increases soldiers' motivation to do hard things. The earlier chapters do exactly that for you, giving you the understanding-based morale and motivation you need to do the things required to help your teenage child to sur-vive and flourish in a challenging world. That's what resilience is all about.

FIVE

Resilience and Its Seven Strategies

Chairs Have Four Legs; Soldiers and Teens Need Seven

I n 1964, U.S. Supreme Court Justice Potter Stewart was apparently up late one night struggling to define pornography when he wrote that he "could never succeed in intelligibly defining porn . . . But I know it when I see it."[1] So it is with resilience, a thing that can be difficult to truly define, yet most of us do think that we "know it when we see it." That's usually when we're watching someone gracefully, calmly, and almost effortlessly handling some adversity that would make most of us nuts. But as you'll see, there is much, much more to resilience.

Resilience and Happiness Go Hand in Hand

Since about forever, experts have wrestled to define what makes up resilience because it's universally found in folks who report being happy in life, which is the ultimate outcome every parent wishes for their child. While the science of "happiness" is a book series in itself, the view relevant to teens is that happy people are not entitled children of rich parents who bubble wrap their kids from any and all stressors (those kids are usually the less happy folks in the world). Even most previously poor lottery winners report that their new millions did not permanently change their overall happiness levels. Researchers find that happiness is only partly related to wealth, and most argue that it seems inversely related to having an easy, stress-free life with a face free of scars.

Psychologist Martin Seligman devised the acronym PERMA to summarize his research-based happiness recipe. He says we humans seem happiest when we have positive emotion (or pleasure, from tasty foods, good music, and so on), engagement (being involved in enjoyable yet challenging activities), relationships (social connections, which are extremely reliable predictors of happiness), meaning (as in "I know what it's all about for me"), and achievement (accomplishment in doing challenging things that often involve failure before success). Folks who report long-term happiness with their lives are usually people who find purpose and passion in their worlds, who struggle sometimes terribly with adversity and reach out to supports to get them through, who sometimes lose but never quit, and who wear their resultant wrinkles and scars with pride. In other words, it does not come from participation trophies. Watching our kids struggle and sometimes lose seems to be too difficult to bear for too many of us new millennium parents. But Grandma had a point when she said, "Whatever doesn't kill you makes you stronger."

Not coincidentally, this happiness research dovetails perfectly with resilience science, both talking about the critical importance of things like empathy, passion, purpose, struggle, and engaging with adversity. I know of two heroes who provide great living examples of the nature of resilience and its payoff of happiness even in the face of horror. These were two combat veterans who had suffered equally catastrophic injuries. Each lost a leg, one the right, the other the left.

I was called for the first case because Andy would not to get out of bed for treatment. He was demanding excessive painkillers, refusing to see his family or girlfriend, and saying that his life was over, he was worthless and unlovable, and he would kill himself at the first opportunity. Eighteen months later, I was called for the second case, which was slightly different. The second soldier, Pete, was also refusing medical advice but by pushing his rehab too hard, refusing appropriate pain meds, begging for extra time in physical therapy, and exhausting himself to a point where the staff worried he might suffer more damage. Andy told me he was no longer the man he used to be and never would be again. Pete told me he had no time to waste to get back to the life he used to have, which included running. This, he explained, was why he was prematurely demanding to get a runner's prosthetic leg.

Perhaps the biggest difference between those two heroes (a title neither will tolerate) was resilience. Many misunderstand that concept as describing someone who meets adversity with steely-eyed coolness and stoicism, never showing pain, fear, hopelessness, or despair—a bulletproof figure standing confidently alone like Gregory Peck in the movie *To Kill a Mockingbird*. (I once saw Peck respond to an interviewer who gushed on about what an amazing man Peck was, an inspiration to always be cool, calm, and unafraid. The interviewer concluded by saying, "I always wanted to be Gregory Peck." "Yeah," Peck sighed, "me too. That guy in the movies.")

When I asked Pete about his incredible positivism, he made the definition of resilience very clear, especially the part about not showing pain or fear. At first he acted as if he didn't understand my question. Then he sighed as if forced to go somewhere he hated and said, "Yeah, OK. I know why you're asking. Yes, what happened to me was horrible." After a pause, his voice got small. "I still get dreams that I hate to tell anyone about. They're so gross I sometimes wake up gagging. I can feel real sorry for myself at times. And the pain can get crazy bad to where I just bawl like a baby. But I won't just sit around and get blown up again. I fight back by reaching out to the people who care about me and I get the support I need to carry on. And part of my healing is from reaching out and helping other vets who got blown up. But no way will I just quit. That f--king war took my leg. I'll be damned before I'll give it another inch of my life. I sh-t you not."

Resilience is not at all about avoiding or not feeling pain, stress, loss, fear, or despair, but rather it's about being able to get back up after the hit. In fact, teen resilience actually requires experiencing scary things but preferably in a graduated dose so the adolescent can slowly build strength, just like with exercise. Many people see resilience as a genetically inherited quality, which some get and some don't, that makes them "tougher." Luckily, research shows that this isn't true, which is great resilience news for parents. It can be learned even by very unresilient adolescents, and it can be fostered through skilled parenting keenly focused upon developing critical teen assets that we'll discuss in a moment.

Parenting for Resilience

"Anyone can love a perfect place. Loving Baltimore
takes some resilience."
—Laura Lippman

I love that quote, an author's insight gifted to me by a parent in a resilience seminar I was doing near Baltimore. Those two short sentences hold two tall truths about resilience and about helping your teen to build it. First, just as Ms. Lippman says of "loving Baltimore," resilience parenting has nothing to do with loving perfect places or people. To the contrary, it is much more about how we lovingly and skillfully help imperfect teens to handle imperfect parts of life while optimistically striving to become better. Second, the quote accurately suggests that raising resilient teenagers requires resilient parents. To raise them well, we must often patiently suffer with our kids' imperfections, not allowing ourselves to rage in our frustration but instead addressing their problems in resilience-building ways that don't crush them with criticism. Yes, this is hard, but as my brother likes to yell in the face of a challenge, "do-a-ble!" You're about to learn how.

That brother made a gazillion dollars in real estate. He once took me to an abandoned village, the most run-down, neglected, and unloved family of old buildings you could imagine. "Don't you love this place?!" he exclaimed.

"Have you lost your mind?" I asked. "This is a mess, nothing but a bunch of problems."

"Yeah, yeah, I know," he impatiently agreed. "But you're only seeing what *is*. The fun is seeing what *can be* in the '*is*.'"

That was a lightning bolt moment for me as an aspiring psychologist and even more as an aspiring parent. Our parental eyes tend to focus upon what our children are not, and that view controls most of what we engage with them about, often in one of two bad ways, both motivated by love. The first is judgmental criticism: "If you weren't such a lazy jerk, maybe you'd amount to something." Many parents think that loving their kid means constantly and painfully reminding them of their failures. The second is when parents go to the other extreme and lavish endless praise upon their kids for things that require no effort and aren't even true, thinking this unconditional affirmation will help the kids master their flaws: "You are the smartest, most talented, and most beautiful girl in that school."

Both types of parenting can crush teen resilience, the first by making them see themselves as hopelessly flawed, and the second by making them think they are innately perfect and thus not required to tolerate the stress and frustration of effort and failure. I once watched one of those "perfect" kids exhaust an already exhausted intern I was supervising via a video feed. The intern's multiple attempts to have this girl own some small portion of her failures were all firmly rebuffed by this client. To this girl, her failures were all caused by the faults of others. I laughed out loud when after 90 minutes of hearing how entitled this girl was, the poor intern lost it. Without hardly moving her lips, she said, "You know, I've been searching for the center of the universe for a long time . . ." I later confessed to the intern that I felt like saying exactly the same thing.

The resilience-building magic is in the middle of those two extremes, a place where we constantly affirm our unshakeable love for our children as they are and still encourage them to build the skills they need to succeed in the world, to become who they can be. We should, as my brother said, be "seeing what 'can be' in the 'is'!"

Several decades of thought, debate, and research have developed a list of resilience components that is roughly agreed upon by experts, a recipe that grew over the years as additional factors were discovered in successful teens. If today you asked 10 different experts for their lists, you'll likely get 11 different ones. I personally like the "Seven Cs of Resilience," a handy distillation offered by Ken Ginsburg in his excellent book *Building Resilience in Children and Teens*. Ken cites his key factors as competence, confidence, connection, character, contribution, coping, and control. (As you'll see, I like to change the order a bit.) In a moment, we'll take a look at what's involved in your parental job of promoting and, more important, not discouraging each of those Cs. Try to keep these lofty goals in mind when trying to survive typical conversations with unresilient teens that can test the resilience of parents. Easy to say, hard to do, even for pros such as me while at a restaurant enjoying some father-daughter bonding time:

"OMG, Dad, look at that woman!" my daughter whispered urgently.

"Where?' I asked as I turned my head.

"OMG, Dad! *Stop looking!*" she loudly hissed. *"You're totally embarrassing me!"*

"But, but, Sarah, you said to . . ."

Sarah was accepting no explanations that day. *"I hate it when you do that!"* she hissed/yelled even louder.

"Do what?" I whispered. "You mean when I look . . . ?"

"No!" she full yelled at me. *"When you yell at me like that!"*

Now all the eyes in the restaurant were upon us, the parenting expert with his surely perfect daughter. "But, but . . ." I quietly pleaded before she firmly ended our father-daughter bonding, now back to her hissing voice: "Just be quiet, Dad,

OK? Before I, like, freak out? Let's just shut up and eat." My appetite was gone. But the wine list sure looked good.

—From the author's personal journal

Tho Sovon Cc of Rooilionoo

1. Competence: There's No Way to Fake a Batting Average

Competence is the ability to handle specific tasks well, a characteristic consisting of many subskills developed from actively engaging with the world, making choices, trusting one's own judgments, taking action, and owning the consequences, good and bad. These are real, definable assets that may be partially innate, but to have value they must be developed through the discipline of work and practice, by getting in the game and winning, and even more by losing. Read on and you'll see how.

COMPETENCE-BUILDING STRATEGIES FOR PARENTS

Strongly Encourage Any/All Activities, Structured or Not

Lots of research says that a teen will develop more competence from unstructured activities than organized ones. Sports and debate teams are great, but even better are your son's "what-a-stupid-waste-of-your-time" rock bands and your daughter's "you-can't-start-your-own-business" ideas. The structured activities are already thought out and mostly directed by adults who essentially tell kids what to do. They'll learn a lot there, but to succeed they only have to do what they're told. Unstructured pursuits will force them to make it up as they go along (creativity) and build other critical life skills, including negotiation, compromise, planning, managing personalities, and most of all, tolerating frustration. If you don't believe that, then you've never had a rock band. Bribe if you must to get your son to try new things (we'll chat more about bribes later in the book). Make him sick of hearing your parental rule about how he spends his time: "You can do most any-thing; you cannot do no-thing."

Say a Lot About What She Does Well, a Little About Her Screwups, and Say It All Smart

You want her to see new activities (aka learning) as exciting adventures—win, lose, or draw. So reinforce all of her efforts but be sure that your positive feedback is truthful and factually based. Use facts such as "You made a great play at third base" and not fluff like "You're the best player in the league." When pointing out a mistake, stay narrowly focused on the one event. Don't say, "You always screw up grounders!" Instead, ask, "If you had that play to do over again, what would you do differently?" Don't stop her thinking with judgmental answers: "You just quit like you always do." Like your kid, whenever I'm criticized, my first reaction is to defend myself, not to think about the issue. Instead, do start her thinking with neutral questions that separate her worth from her actions: "What do you think went wrong?"

Let Her Make (Nonlethal) Mistakes

Here's another parenting mantra for you: *A bad decision made well is better than a good decision made poorly.* The best learning is not from positive outcomes but from positive decision-making processes. Parents who take over and direct their kid's decisions to ensure success (the good decision made poorly) rob their child of the most important part: the decision-making practice. Wise parents (the ones with tongues that are sore from being bitten) shut up and let their kids decide as much as safely possible, especially when they're headed for a clear failure. Remember, resilience learning comes from handling life's negatives, not from being insulated from them.

> At age 13, my gifted son decided that social studies was "ir- relevant to my lifestyle" and "clearly a government attempt at mind control for the masses" in which he was refusing to participate. He seemed certain the teacher would never fail someone as smart as him. To no avail, we debated the wis- dom of this, and then my wife and I bit our tongues and de- cided to let him decide, despite the looks we got at parent-teacher conferences. He was absolutely furious when he was finally told he was getting an F on his report card. This was a consequence my wife and I declined to appeal in a meeting where the nervous teacher offered us that option. We were stunned when he quietly confided that in his nine years of teaching, we were his first parents of a failing stu- dent to not argue for a better grade for their child. A decade later, that same kid graduated from college with honors. Knowing my son a bit, I believe that if we took over his decision-making process in middle school, he might not have ever wanted to figure out how to get As in college.
>
> —From the author's personal journal

That was one of those 10,000 tough, vague, no-easy-answer par- enting decisions where you have to choose your mission (to control your kid or to teach him to control himself) and then select the best strategy and tactic for your particular child. If it helps you to tolerate his F, think about your own life for a minute. When did you do your best learning: in your successes or in your failures? Personally, I don't recall many of my successes, but I can tell you about my screwups in excruciating detail. I keep them in the front of my head where they constantly whisper, "Want to feel like that again? Then be smarter this time."

2. Confidence: Projecting Competence into the Future

Confidence is a quiet, positive belief in one's future based upon feeling good about past efforts, successful or not. As Megan reminded me, that's because success lives in the effort, not the outcome:

> Megan was a mass of bruises, scratches, and fatigue from head to toe. The day before, this 16-year-old girl had lost a heartbreaking rugby playoff game. "We lost to them twice in the regular season, by like 40 points, no joke. They were mad bigger and faster than us. We called them 'the Amazons.' But this time, this time we played them tough. We had three goal line stands where we held them off. We were tied until they scored with two minutes to go. Then we drove to like their 10-yard line. Everyone on the sidelines was screaming. We just knew we were gonna win. And then . . . ," her voice trailed off with a deep sigh, "I made a bad toss and time ran out. It was pretty horrible." I worried that she was terribly crushed. "Megan, what are you feeling?" I asked. "You look so sad. Are you done with rugby?" That's when she reminded me of what was important. "Why would I do that?" she asked incredulously. "Because I said it

was horrible? It was horrible. And it was incredible! They never had a close game all season and they were so scared of us. That was great! I can't freaking wait till next year!"

CONFIDENCE-BUILDING STRATEGIES FOR PARENTS

Expect the Best of Your Child's Characteristics

Don't expect the best of your child's achievements but of her personal qualities such as integrity, persistence, and compassion. When those assets are in place, achievement becomes hard to stop and confidence just about impossible to kill. When those things are missing, success means little. So be sure to have your priority list straight. Those expectations are important when your kid is doing great, and more important when she's going crazy, a time when we often lower our expectations and focus only upon survival.

Remember back in Chapter 3 where you learned that psychologically speaking, everyone can be viewed as not one but three different people (the {P}-{A}-{C} brain system)? Use that lens to help you and your kid to see her craziness as being driven by the temporarily raging emotions of her {C} brain overrunning the smart thoughts in her {A} brain. This helps you and her to see these behaviors as symptoms, not sins—as painful tendencies to be corrected over time, not as character flaws of which to be forever ashamed. If they'll allow it, a good line of questions following a terrible decision by teens is:

- "I know you're better than that. What was your {C} brain saying to do?"
- "What was your {A} brain suggesting?"
- "Which is who you want to be?"

See Mistakes as Success Ingredients, Not Stupidity

For yourself and your kid, frame his mistakes not simply as screwups but as part of a normal learning process toward good decision making. Do this especially with those particular mistakes that recur many times. See his errors not as demoralizing failures but as the steps of learning needed for eventual success. Seeing setbacks in that light builds confidence by reducing the fear of future risk and failure. Seeing setbacks as things of which to be ashamed crushes confidence and powerfully argues for never trying again. So after your kid screws up, yet again, say things such as, "Every single pitcher in the major leagues learned to hit strike zones by first hitting siding, windows, and his father's big toes."

Praise More for Effort than for Success

Success on an easy task promotes little confidence, and if overly praised, it can create a tendency to seek only more easy tasks. Ease back on praising easy wins and praise the heck out of hard-fought losses: "I am so incredibly impressed with how hard you played especially after being down so many points. When folks try that hard at everything they do, they win a lot more than they lose. And when they lose, they only lose that one contest. They never, ever lose their pride."

What we call laziness is often fear of losing expressed in a crippling way. Many of us think it hurts less to lose if we don't really try than to lose after giving it our all. Help her learn about this by asking her questions to zero in on the real fear. Use that {P}-{A}-{C} system:

Parent: "What stops you from studying?"
Teen: "I get kinda nervous and can't focus, and I play on my phone instead."

Parent: "What bad thing could happen if you study?"
[Make her run her answer list by repeating "So?" until
she gets to the real deal at the end of her list.]

Teen: "I'm scared I'll fail the test."

Parent: "So?"

Teen: "Kids will laugh at me."

Parent: "So?"

Teen: "I'll feel stupid 'cause I tried hard and still messed up."

Parent: "Then you think it's more painful to fail after really
trying than after not trying? You think that you should
just flunk yourself before the test flunks you? Which brain
is saying that, your 4-year-old brain or your 14-year-old
brain?"

Teen: "I guess my 4-year-old."

Parent: "What does your 14-year-old brain say?"

Teen: "It says I should try 'cause if I don't I'll never succeed."

Parent: "I guess you'll have to decide which of your brains
is smarter."

3. Connection: If You Must Pick Only One of the Seven Cs of Resilience . . .

. . . pick this one. Kids who feel safe and secure in their most
powerful relationships *are* safe and secure, tending to be much
less crazy in their behaviors and reporting much less stress in
their lives. Your teen's most powerful relationship is with you,
his parent. Research consistently shows that we have more real
impact on our children than any other force in their world, for
better and for worse. In Part III, we'll give you the tactics you
need to maintain a close, loving relationship with him during the

same conversation in which he's screaming because you won't allow him to attend a beer party in the park. But first, let's look at some strategies to build a connection so strong that it can calm the storms of adolescence that can rage in your home. Those storms also rage in prisons:

As a terrified, skinny new staffer working in a very violent juvenile forensic unit (a prison for teenagers), I attached myself to a veteran shrink named Gene who was later to become my teacher, mentor, and hero. Mondays were the most dangerous days since the weekend staff sometimes incorrectly placed extremely dangerous new inmates in less secure wards. One such Monday, we were called "code red" to a large cafeteria where a new kid was snapping out. He was huge—"scared and scarred," as Gene would say, and thus very dangerous. He was also standing on a counter, screaming death threats and swinging an industrial-grade mop handle at the skull of anyone who approached. Surrounded by about 20 Ph.D.'s and 10 muscled guards trying to talk him down, he was not impressed with the degrees or the muscles. He was ready to die to make some point. We watched helplessly as the guards got ready to rush and take him down, which meant bad things were likely to happen.

Suddenly, an old but firm voice rang out from behind us: "Ronald! What *are* you doing, boy?"

We turned to see the least credentialed or muscled adult in the room, a woman of perhaps 70 pushing a maintenance cart. The room fell silent as Ronald froze in place. "What did I tell you, boy?" she asked as she limped slowly past us. "I *told* you, son, you *got* to play by the rules here. Those boys over there," she pointed to the guards, "those boys will *kill* you, son. They love this stuff." She was now at his feet looking up at him. "Give me that," she ordered, stretching out her weathered hand. Ronald handed over the weapon as she offered her other hand. "Now, get down from there and stop all this nonsense."

Ronald slowly placed his hand in hers and hopped down, and she casually escorted him to the ward where she knew he belonged. We heard her voice fading down the hall as she lectured him on the way: "I told you, didn't I? You'll be safe if you just calm down . . ." We later learned that she had befriended this terrified kid over the weekend and somehow made a magical connection with him. But Gene surmised all this on the spot. He turned to me and said, "You just witnessed the neurological power of a respect-based, caring connection."

—From the author's personal journal

CONNECTION-BUILDING STRATEGIES FOR PARENTS

Make Your Home the Safe Port in Stormy Seas

In Part I, we saw how a teenager navigating today's world is pretty much a poorly equipped boat (shaky brain) caught in an ocean storm (threatening culture). Make your home a place where she can expect safety and security by eliminating the verbal violence of your own yelling and threatening even as you conflict with him. Above all else, be sure that physical violence (slapping, punching, and so on) is never even considered regardless of the degree of his provocations. Always easy to say, often hard to do.

Love Her Especially When You "Hate" Her

She must know in her heart that the conflict she feels from you is about her *behavior* and not about *her*. During the bad times, use one of my favorite statements when she screams that you don't love her: "I'm so sorry it feels that way, and I'd like to hear about why it does. But know that no matter what you do, you are not able to ever make me stop loving you. You cannot make that happen." Show her how, contrary to the myth, love and "hate" can sort of coexist, at least in parenting: "I hate that decision you made that hurt you. I also love you way too much to let you think that what you did was OK."

Allow Him to Express All of His Emotions, Including the Ones You Don't Want to Hear

A key to closeness with adolescents is giving them permission to say what they feel straight up without them worrying about losing your love. If he can tell you he hates you, then you can take it to the bank when he says that he loves you. In that way, like with publicity, communication is never "good" or "bad." It's all communication, as long as it's not abusive.

Be Like the Assassin: Separate the "Business" from the "Personal"

Remember that whatever you do, your teen is watching you like a hawk, absorbing all she sees you do and little of what you say she should do. That fact scares the heck out of me too. So when it comes to things such as conflicting with your life partner (or other close folks), be sure your teen sees you maintaining that connection of love even while powerfully disagreeing. This separates the issue from the relationship and often even offers a kindness amid the conflict: *"You left the burner on again and ruined my best pot! What do I have to do to get you to remember that?"* Pause for deep breath. "Sorry. I shouldn't have yelled. It's just a pot. By the way, I'm making coffee. Want some?" Let your daughter see over and over that conflict does not have to mean loss of love. Borrow a trick from the assassins (at least the ones on TV). "Sorry, buddy. Nothin' personal. Just business."

4. Character: What You Do When No One's Looking

To a worrisome extent, many of today's teens report having no idea about what character is about or why it's so important, which it is in two ways. The first way has to do with the world, both the one on your block and the one on the planet. Try to imagine the world without high-character people. Delete every "good deed" story from the Internet and consider what would be left. OMG, right?

The second way has to do with the vital importance of character as a core ingredient in resilient teens. We've already seen how a long decline of character traits seems to be one of the factors critical to teenage suffering as compared to that of past generations of adolescents, such as those in 1970. Back then, a group called Crosby, Stills, Nash & Young sang in "Teach Your Children" that your kids " . . . must have a code that you can live by, and so become yourself . . ." Today's resilience researchers could not have said that any better. Multiple studies prove that having character, a core set of beliefs about right and wrong, is incredibly powerful in building teen resilience by helping them be guided by their own beliefs and not those of others. That is indeed the path to becoming yourself.

In adolescence, we call that process *identity consolidation*, knowing who you are and how you fit in your world. Once that magic happens, teens are much better at decision making, feel comfortable with themselves (have self-worth), are more confident, and report feeling less stress. Not a bad set of payoffs from a little character. Building character in a teen in today's world can sometimes seem flat-out hopeless. However, it turns out that all you have to do is have a little faith and keep doing the right thing, especially when it seems hopeless. Did you know that Winston Churchill had five kids, four of whom were daughters? That's how I know he was not talking about World War II when he said, "If you're going through hell, keep going." I think David would agree:

David felt hopeless—and furious. Up to now, he had shown only his anger. This was a guy who, even by his daughter Erin's account, cared nothing for himself. Instead, he spent all of his time and energy taking care of everyone else, including and especially her. His "reward" was discovering that this 14-year-old girl was not only sexting with a number of boys but was also having casual sex. In a session I had with them both, David admitted that when he found out what was happening, he had screamed at her since she seemed to not "give a damn about the morality of all this." When I asked him what feeling preceded his anger when he found out, he sat for a minute as his anger slowly faded. "I guess—hurt?" he offered. "I was—I still am devastated. I thought she was better than that. I thought she valued herself better than that, and now . . . now she doesn't even care about herself. That's not what we taught her, not what we talked about with her all her life. I don't know who she is."

Erin stared at the floor as tears filled her eyes. "Erin," I asked softly, "how do you feel about what you've been doing?" She bit her lip for a long time and then in a shaking voice said, "I feel horrible. I feel so ashamed when I even think of it, I want to not be alive. That's why I couldn't talk about it with him."

David exploded. *"Then why the hell did you . . ."* but she exploded right back: *"I don't know why, OK? I just don't! But I do know I feel crummy, and I know that's not how I want to be!* It's not who I want to be." After a minute of painful silence, she added, "Dad, just because I don't do what you say, that doesn't mean I don't listen to you or that I don't respect what you say. I do listen. And I do respect you. It just gets, I don't know, confusing, you know?"

David slowly nodded as if he had just learned something important.

OK, maybe you have to have a *lot* of faith through the dark days when your child's code seems nothing like your code. But remember the last verse of that old Crosby, Stills, Nash & Young song:

> *"Teach your parents well,*
> *Their children's hell will slowly go by,*
> *And feed them on your dreams*
> *The one they pick's the one you'll know by."*

What kids do now is not what they will do forever if they and their parents can learn to listen to each other. That's how character gets formed.

CHARACTER-BUILDING STRATEGIES
FOR PARENTS

Show the Power of Character on Others

Ask your kid to name someone he knows personally whom he admires and respects. He won't name you even though that's likely the first name that pops in his head (he will name you when he's 25). When he says "my coach" or "Grandma," then ask what exactly he admires and respects about that person. You'll hear a list of how that person gives so much of himself and really cares about others. Then ask your son, "When you're around that person, does that ever change the way you feel, the way you act, the way you see the world? How do you explain that?"

Then, throw a pebble in the pond and show how one behavior ripples out in every direction, having impacts that are often hard to see, both good and bad. Mention that we each have the choice of what kind of pebbles to toss, though usually we don't get to see where or how far the ripples go. Use a real example of this for him with his own "pebble": "This morning I saw you being patient with your little sister, and you know what? After you left, I watched her actually be sweet to the baby who makes her feel so jealous. You have no idea how happy and proud you made me. I hope you are proud of you."

Show the Power of Character on Self

Share with her what your character does for you. Reflect and think about your proudest personal life moments and what those character moments bring to you now, how doing the right thing gets us out of our own self-centered heads and helps us feel good. Then share the "Hero's Dilemma," which teaches how personal and sacred a thing character really is, of how it becomes less sacred the more it becomes publicly celebrated. "I can recall moments in dark days when I did the right thing and no one knew but me. The strange thing is that those acts felt less important the more that people found out."

You can also tell her about Gino Bartali, a champion cyclist from Italy who hid his Jewish friend and the friend's family from the fascists during World War II. Moreover, Bartali repeatedly risked his life by becoming a courier for a secret network set up to hide Jews and help them escape from Italy, instead of being rounded up and sent to concentration camps. He helped hundreds of Jews survive. After the war, he wanted no one to know of his heroism. His son recounts the story of discovering the amazing truth and then being ordered by his father not to share it: "When I asked my father why I couldn't tell anyone, he said, 'You must do good, but you must not talk about it. If you talk about it you're taking advantage of other's misfortunes for your own gain.'"

Help Him Find Purpose and Meaning in Life

This is another character strategy that is best done with questions, not answers. Find those small windows of calm (often bought with a bribe to share mocha lattes at the coffee shop) to lob large questions at him: "What is life all about, for you?" and "What do you think you will value about your life at the end of it?" Do a bunch of these latte mini-chats over the years to help him slowly identify his values. His immediate answers are actually not important, and all you may hear are sarcastic ones, but that's all OK. Remember that good parenting is largely guerilla warfare. That's where you don't fight nose-to-nose Gettysburg style (that didn't work out so good) but rather run up to your opponent's wall, lob a grenade over, and then run the hell away.

Your grenades should be well-framed questions that you lob into your kid's brain, and then let it go. If you argue or judge, your kid will think only about winning the argument, not mulling your question. If you want more impact, say less.

5. Control: Grant Me the Serenity . . .

Whether you are religious or not, one of the best requests you can make of whomever/whatever you talk with in the sky is captured in the Serenity Prayer written by theologian Reinhold Niebuhr in the mid-1900s. It has many versions but this is the one my teen clients like:

> *"Grant me the serenity to accept the things I cannot change,*
> *the courage to change the things I can,*
> *and the wisdom to know the difference."*

You'd think that Niebuhr guy would have been on Oprah, since he packed so much smart stuff about control into so little a space. As we saw in Part I, a key marker of this generation of teens is their historically low sense of control over the outcomes of their lives or their ability to impact the world around them. That pessimistic belief is a virus that can cause passiveness, depression, and anxiety in your kid, all things that kill resilience. Conversely, the teen who thinks she does have significant control over her life and her corner of the world is perpetually optimistic, seeing setbacks as things to be energetically attacked anew, not as depressing confirmations of the hopelessness of existence.

CONTROL-BUILDING STRATEGIES FOR PARENTS

Provide Color Commentary

When you talk about the events he witnesses, you can show how in life most things happen as the direct result of someone's choices and actions. For example, when he's calmed down from screaming at the TV about the football gods conspiring against his hopeless team, quietly ask if there were any choices and actions involved in that loss for his team and in that win for the opponent (aside from the gods' conspiracy). Again, lob a "grenade" question into his brain about what would now work best for his team's coach: to darkly ruminate about unbeatable football gods or to watch the tape to see what choices and actions caused the loss and, done over, could bring a win next time.

Constantly Point Out Their Successes

That way, they hear some counterpoint to what they mostly hear about all day, namely their failures. In their eight hours of hearing from folks such as bus drivers ("You walk like an old man!"), teachers ("You studied the wrong chapter!"), boyfriends or girlfriends ("You don't care about me!"), and coaches ("Get your head out of your butt!"), teens get worn down by nonstop criticism just like the rest of us. A difference is that they often lack the resilience of adults who can take steps to balance things for themselves. Non-resilient teens can get criticized into a state of hopelessness where they take the negatives into their hearts and begin to lose the ability to accept or even really hear positives. If the only news channel they can get is WWWY (What's Wrong With You), their pessimism can become permanent, and control becomes only what adults do to them.

Always Link Autonomy with Responsibility

When negotiating privileges (curfews, phones, and so on), make it clear that the power is always in their hands to get what they want by making responsible choices, and that they have control over their lives based upon their choices and actions. Avoid punishments where they have no control over an outcome that is announced after they screw up: "You're late! You're grounded tomorrow!" Instead, use consequences where they know in advance the possible outcomes as determined by their choices and actions: "If you're home on time tonight, you earn the privilege of going out tomorrow. If not, you don't. OK?"

Model That Serenity Prayer

Acknowledge and affirm the hopelessness and sadness he can see in the world, and then point him toward healing actions using yourself as an example: "Yes, that bombing was truly horrific. I can't begin to imagine how that was for those parents to lose their children. There surely is evil in the world. You know, I feel like pushing back against the bad a bit. Want to come with me to help at the food bank? I can't rescue those children who died but maybe I can help a few not go hungry tonight. I know it's weird. It doesn't sound like much but it sure helps me handle the horrors. I guess it's good to focus on what I can control, even if it's a small thing."

Begin a Pile of Pebbles

Grab another pebble, but don't toss it; just lay it down. Then put another on top. And another. Then ask what there would be if millions of people each added only one pebble: "Yeah, sweetie, I hear you. The fact that we only fed two families doesn't seem like much compared to what happened in that bombing. But what if everyone in the world who could all fed two hungry families tonight? How might the world be different? And you know, what seems so small to you might not seem so small to those kids who are going to eat well tonight. Ain't life strange? Seems like it's mostly changed one pebble at a time."

6. Coping: Rolling with the Punches

Resilience is not about never getting punched by life. It's about how well we roll with those punches that will come. The resilience strategy of coping—or developing coping skills—is about first being in shape to absorb some hits with minimal damage (wellness), and then healing from the big hits to get back into the game as quickly as possible.

COPING SKILLS-BUILDING STRATEGIES FOR PARENTS

Model Wellness, Don't Compel It

When I become king of the world (still waiting for that call), edict number two will be that all teenagers get adequate exercise, good nutrition, (and proper sleep as per edict number one). Of course, if I did that my fellow psychologists would have me killed since my edicts would put most of us out of business. Because when it comes to adolescents, much of what we diagnose, treat, and powerfully medicate as anxiety, depression, and ADHD is actually poor lifestyle.

Before you blame "pill-pushing psychiatrists" (actually, most see meds as a last resort), know that when parents bring their teens into my office for a diagnosis that will get pills for their kids, their eyes often glaze over if I suggest trying a few radical treatments before turning to medications. Radical treatments such as walking around the block a few times a day, eating something green once in a while, and—most extreme of all—getting nine hours of sleep . . . without electronic screens in the room. Over the top, right? Often, those parents say they'll call back about the next appointment, and then they go down the block to find someone else from whom to get the pills. Before you blame those parents, know that they already realize that exercise, nutrition, and sleep can make a huge difference, but they have found that screaming at their kid to get well doesn't work well, and thus meds look like the only option.

You'll have to wait until Part III to get the full drill on promoting teen wellness, but for now know that silently modeling it is the most effective method. Trying to force it becomes another parent versus teen football game where the issue of wellness gets lost in the fight to win the game. Want her to hate wellness? Try compelling it.

Use Coaching, Not Bubble Wrap

If you manage to insulate teenagers from all stress, you'll deprive them of the life-saving experience of being stressed and overcoming it. Remember when we discussed that too much and too little stress were both terrible for your kid? We humans are at our best when appropriately stressed, like when we play the game having no idea whether or not we'll win. Playing an overwhelming team (excessive stress) is crushing. Playing an underwhelming team (inadequate stress) is boring. The evenly matched contest (appropriate levels of stress)? Now there's a game! Stop viewing all of your kid's stressors as viruses. Instead, look at them as stress vaccinations, weakened versions that slowly build her up to handle the real deals when they hit. Use that {P}-{A}-{C} personality system to help her to organize her own thoughts and emotions to make analyses and action plans. View that demanding classroom as her emotional gym, helping her to strengthen for the next level of challenge.

Narrate Your Own Coping Skills for Them to Hear

When you're under the gun, become a little weird and talk aloud to yourself to really talk aloud to him: "That deadline is really stressing me out right now. Feels like I can't do this and that I should just quit. But that's just my four-year-old brain whining. I know in my adult brain that I can get this done. No way will I let fear make my decisions. My quit-because-I'm-afraid decisions were the worst mistakes of my life."

7. Contribution: Improving Ourselves by Improving the World

Before the days of video cameras, I once worked in a school where vandalism ran wild, and the effect was crippling that sad community. All of our control efforts failed until a brand-new art teacher suggested, "Why don't we make this their place? Let's get the kids to decorate it themselves. Maybe they won't trash their own house." Over time, giving up some control proved to be the best control method of all. The quality of the creative murals and the power of the motivational quotes that quickly proliferated all over the walls were way beyond the expectations of the adults.

One morning as I entered and caught the familiar depressing smell of graffiti spray paint, I heard a kid's voice admonishing the vandal: "Yo! Dude!! This is *my* school!" Think for a minute about the immeasurable resilience-building magic in those six little words. In them you can find competence (knowing how to assert), confidence (standing up to a jerk), connection (caring for the community), character (knowing what's right), control (realizing the capability of impacting upon an environment), and coping (finding a great way to address a stress/depression issue). In resilience parenting, contribution does indeed put it all together.

CONTRIBUTION-BUILDING STRATEGIES FOR PARENTS

If You Live in Disney World, Keep the Real World Close

If you're fortunate enough to live in Disney World (that is, you're well off), never let your kid forget that blessing, but do it softly as an observation on your whole family and not to put her down as an entitled teen: "We are so incredibly lucky to live as we do, to have all we need. Makes me feel a tad guilty and sad for those who don't." Be sure to point out that real world is always right around the corner, needing all the help it can get.

Think Out Loud Again, but About Your Own Contribution Process

Say something like: "I'd love to play golf today, but after seeing the line at the shelter, I couldn't enjoy it. Hey, want to take a ride with me? I think I'll drop off that money as a donation instead. You know, something that maybe does more for me than for them? It's weird, but the last time I did this I remember feeling sorry for myself on the way there. On the way back, I couldn't believe I had been whining about that. I was just happy."

Beg, Borrow, or Bribe to Get Your Teen Contributing

Some kids are born contributors. Others need a push to begin to understand the magic. In the end, even the jerks benefit. Actually, they can benefit more:

This 17-year-old was not the arrogant, self-centered gift to creation who had sat in my office two months prior. He took up less space, sitting upright on the couch, this time not splayed all over it. His sneering, I-know-it-all smirk was gone. His voice was softer. He looked so much wiser. He could even be silent a bit. And he was thinner. "My parents, like, bribed me to go on that mission trip," he said as he sat forward. "Promised me I would get my license if I'd go. You *know* how bad I wanted that, right? So I went, but it was, like—like nothing I expected." He studied his sunburned, newly roughened hands. "We helped build a school and a clinic in these, like, ghetto villages. Not 'ghetto,' that's dumb. I mean—poor, you know? Really poor. We stayed with these families, you know, and they would feed us. After a couple of meals, we figured out that most of these families, they would put out like every bit of decent food they had for us, and they would like sort of pretend to eat until they were sure that we ate all we wanted. Before we figured that out, I used to eat up their food like a pig, like they could just run to the store to get more, you know, like it is here." He shook his head. "This one family? I accidentally caught them putting away the good food after I left, and they were going to eat the not good stuff. And when I walked in on them, *they* acted embarrassed in front of me!" Now his head hung down. "Man, I was the one who should have been embarrassed. I felt like such a jerk. I feel like such a jerk."

Feeling like "such a jerk" has always preceded growth for me. How about you? Well, same for our kids.

Community: Another C of Resilience

Some resilience experts also include *community* on their lists of the Cs of resilience, since it is so important. Research powerfully shows that kids who interact positively and significantly with their communities (families, neighborhoods, towns, schools, religious centers) are much more resilient and less stressed. That interaction is magical when it is a give-and-take of mutual support and caring, by a bunch of folks contributing back and forth. The magic is that if you get your kid to give away a piece of herself, it comes back to her—with interest:

"You know how horrible I feel about myself, about being the biggest loser in 10th grade? Well, no offense, but I found something that works better than counseling." For the first time in the month that I had worked with her, Melissa did look as if maybe she was not quite the loser she had thought. "I spent the weekend working at the Special Olympics for my [school-required community service] hours. I started out scared to even show up. I was just waiting to get put down by the other kids from my school I knew would be there. And then I started working with those little kids who have these incredible challenges. And they mostly all were so happy and excited, and they didn't care what anyone thought about them. At the end, this one girl I had been helping out—she didn't even know how to talk, you know? She would just make these noises. Anyway, at the end, she ran up to me and gave me this huge hug and made this like cooing sound. Some kids were staring and I just didn't care! I knew exactly what she was saying and that's all that mattered." Melissa thought for a moment. "Something big happened there, for me. That day I went home not caring what the other kids from my school thought about me. It, like, just wasn't that important anymore. And that lasted for a few days. Maybe if I keep doing that stuff, then maybe I won't worry so much."

So before you plunk down a load of money for counseling, try a little community contribution treatment with your teen. Even if you have to bribe to get her there, it's likely cheaper than therapy. And, like Melissa said, it can be more effective.

And there you go! You have developed your mission of building your kid's resilience, a mission defined by information about teenagers and their anti-resilience brains and world. This chapter taught you the strategies you need to make them strong, to fulfill that mission. Now all you need are the specifics about how to do all that in your day-to-day parenting—training known as tactics.

SIX

Tactics

The Day-to-Day of How It Works
(and How It Never Works)

Martha was weary of dealing with her 15-year-old daughter. "Just when you think you've got this parenting thing down, everything blows up again, and we all go back to start. Abbey changes at warp speed. After a year of fighting over TV—you know, where Abbey 'would die' without one in her room—she now has started demanding that her boyfriend be allowed to sleep over. I didn't even know she had a boyfriend! She swore to me that they would never have sex or anything like that. When I gave her my wide-eyed 'you have lobsters crawling out of your ears' look, she calmly pointed out that my 'sex' worry only occurs to me because my mom mind 'is like always in the gutter.' That made me see more lobsters." She paused to chuckle at her own joke, a very good therapeutic sign. "Dr. B, I think parenting a teenager is like that poker game where the dealer calls the game: The rules keep changing and you're always trying to play catch up. Abbey never stays still long enough so one set of rules works. I guess playing smart poker involves more than just having rules."

"Yep," I answered. "It's time to chat about tactics."

Tactics vs. Rules

Martha's words are a great preface to the tactics you are about to learn. Rules are codes or laws that essentially say "If you break this rule, the following punishment will happen." Simple rules and punishments might have worked back in the day for the old parent mission for the old war (namely, to control teen behavior). Our new mission for this new war (teaching our children to control themselves) needs so much more than rules: It needs tactics. Tactics are guidelines to be thoughtfully adapted to the unique needs of each teen, even within one set of sibs sharing the same gene pool. Rules that may have worked great for your compliant older son can seem to be only detonation devices to your younger daughter.

Teens are endlessly changing, morphing from one creature to another, sometimes almost overnight. Picture those human evolution video shorts showing an amoeba becoming Albert Einstein in 30 seconds and you get the idea of adolescence. The hard part is parenting the hundred mutations that present along the way. You see, teens passionately feel as if each one of those evolutionary stages is their final developmental destination, that this is who they'll be forever, and that you are so unfair to not accept their new and forever persona. As solidly "finished" as you might feel as a human being at 50, teens feel just as passionately that they'll never, ever change their present core beliefs (which might be their third major shift in a week). Late at night, when a teen is not taking part in any particular fight over an issue, his underdeveloped {A} brain sometimes softly concedes that he is likely to keep changing. But that miraculous, quiet insight does little to calm his {C} brain's overwhelming and often consuming passion over things such as boyfriends/girlfriends, drugs/alcohol, or even vocational goals:

Brian was a great 16-year-old. Up to now, he had presented hardly a lick of trouble to his parents, got As in challenging courses at school, and participated in lots of activities. "My parents are, like, major freaked about my dropping out of 11th grade, like I've gone insane," he said. "They sent me here because they think I need meds or something. They keep yelling about all the AP courses I took and how I'll be wasting all of that time and effort and everything. They act like I don't have a plan or anything. I do. I showed it to them. I even created spreadsheets. I've thought this out very carefully and researched it a lot. My dad, he keeps asking me what I'm running from. I'm not running from anything; I'm running toward my life goal! School is OK, but it's not for me anymore. I've outgrown wanting to be a biomedical engineer. Now I know what I want to do with the rest of my life. Why can't they be happy and just support me?"

Brian's parents had brought him to me for an evaluation following Brian's PowerPoint presentation to them about his new vocational passion and his plan to achieve it. He was going to drop out of school, hitchhike across the country to California, and live by scavenging the beaches with a metal detector while he learned how to surf, then he would eventually manage a surf shop. "Do you know how great those beach

scavenger guys make out?" he asked me earnestly. I was
afraid to ask.

You can likely imagine what Brian's parents' "our-mission-is-to-control" response sounded like. You'd be very close if you guessed *"Are you out of your freaking mind? We'll have you arrested first!"* You can likely also imagine what his "I'm-an-adult-you-can't-tell-me-what-to-do" response sounded like. You'd be very close again if you also guessed that Brian silently vowed, "I'll just sneak out one night and they'll never catch me." This is what happens when you attack someone's passions and beliefs, especially those belonging to a teenager. How are we adults when people angrily attack and denigrate ours? Are we thoughtful and reflective, weighing the possible wisdom in their words, or are we instantly and royally pissed off, thinking only about counterattacking? Right. And we're all grown up. Mostly.

As you'll see both in this chapter and in Part III (where there are specific applications of the strategies and tactics), the rules you'll devise for your kids are simply temporary leash lines that must constantly be adjusted to the needs and capabilities of each child, always keeping the new mission in mind. So rules are not what you need from me. At best, rules to control behavior are neutrally observed by your kid's {A} brain. At worst, they breed resentment, anger, and rebellion in his {C} brain. Conversely, resilience-building tactics can teach forever. Think of tactics as processes through which you and your kid can keep writing and rewriting rules in ways that build resilience.

10 Terrific Tactics for Resilience Parenting

1. Discipline Smart: Being the Calm Cop When Your Kid Screws Up

Responding skillfully to the conflict situations that are bound to arise with your teen is greatly involved in achieving each of the seven resilience-building strategies we talked about in Chapter 5. Conflict on its own is not only OK in a parenting relationship— it's actually critical in helping your kid learn how to resolve problems without locking and loading. In the proper dose and tone, conflict is therapeutic and resilience-building. In the improper dose and tone, it's a toxin to building resilience.

For example, how do you feel about cops? Remember the time you got a ticket from an angry police officer for blowing a stop sign? You know, that big, loud, sarcastic, intimidating, insulting guy who just about threw the ticket in the window at you, saying, "Yeah, yeah, lady, I know. The gas pedal got stuck, right?" He intentionally took lots of time writing you up so that you would be even more late to work, and then he told you that might teach you a lesson. How did you feel? Who were you mad at? The cop! When you got home, what did you tell your partner? You were likely raving about the cop's demeanor, saying he was crazy and shouldn't be a cop or allowed to carry a gun. You were obsessed with wanting to strike back and make him feel crummy for having made you feel crummy, so you did the worst safe thing you could: You wrote a complaint letter about him, knowing nothing would come of it but just wanting to hurt him back. And the next day, when you came to that same stop sign and saw that same cop staring at you, didn't you get a weird suicidal impulse in the back of your head to maybe cruise through that sign a little bit just to mess with him? Of course, since you're not an adolescent you likely were able to get your {A} brain to veto that {C} urge.

About a month later, you got pulled over again for that same offense, but this time by a different cop with a different manner. "Sorry, ma'am," she began. "I'm afraid you missed that stop sign back there. By your mirror tag I see that you're a teacher at the high school so I know you're late. I'll get you out of here as soon as I can. Be right back." She quickly returned with the exact same ticket with the same points and fines as the ticket written by that first angry cop, but she presented it a little differently: "Ma'am, this is a terrible intersection. About twice a year we get to pick up body parts here and I'd rather those not be yours." As she handed you the ticket, she calmly said, "Here you go. Please allow yourself enough time or at least slow down. I've seen first-hand that it's truly better to get to work late than not at all. I hope the rest of your day is better than this. Take care." As she walked away, whom were you mad at? And when you got home, did you rant to your partner about the cop or about your own out-of-control schedule that you've got to fix so you don't kill someone?

PUNISHMENTS VS. CONSEQUENCES

Punishments are where we hurt someone for being harmful (disrespectful, uncaring, unsafe, rebellious), which mostly just makes the punished person want to hurt someone more. That first, angry cop used punishment. He was either having a really bad day or he truly believed that making people feel crummy (hurt, sad, scared) helps them make better decisions. Parental punishments are usually constructed on the spot, when we're the ones who are hurt/scared/mad, often at 2 AM, and often communicated with denigration and rage. They often are so over the top that we rarely enforce them. This inconsistency, of course, makes them worse than useless as parenting tools. Punishments can also set up vicious circle retaliations that can go on for years like little wars. They are not our best work:

Parent (loudly): *"You ungrateful little bitch! You need to grow the hell up! You're grounded until your first child graduates from college, assuming I let you live that long!"*

Teen (silently): "Oh yeah? She thinks grounding me hurts? Wait till she sees that her 'bitch' daughter has changed the password on her precious work computer! What's she gonna do then? Ground me forever?"

Punishments can lead to contests of craziness that parents usually lose since it's hard to out-crazy a lunatic terrorist. When it's fired up, your teen's {C} brain is essentially willing to die to make a point. You likely are not.

Parent: *"If you don't unlock my laptop, I'm taking the door off your bedroom!"*

Teen: *"Knock yourself the f--k out! And save some time and take out the carpets and floorboards while you're there since I'll be erasing your hard drive first chance I get."*

Exactly what does a parent do then? Call the Central Intelligence Agency for instructions on waterboarding? Personally, I've tried that but they refused to accept my argument that I was truly dealing with a terrorist. One sympathetic agent was a veteran parent of a teenage daughter. Before she hung up, she said, "Your daughter's 14? You poor bastard!"

Punishments trigger the {C} brains and shut down the {A} brains inside of everyone, but especially teenagers. They can sometimes control specific behaviors for a time, but they can teach only what *not* to do when the punisher is around in order to avoid more pain. Punishments can't teach what *to* do as being the right thing to do.

Consequences are where we set up an outcome for an action that has been previously agreed upon (or at least previously discussed) before the action has occurred. The trick is calmly placing the power in your kid's hands to make his own choices to dictate his own future, knowing that his choices will cause the outcome—not your anger. Consequences are entirely different from punishments although they can look the same to the unskilled observer. The key is in the tone of delivery and in the pre-knowledge of the subject.

As you flash by some poor soul on the roadside getting a ticket, all you know is that she's getting a ticket. You don't know if she got a consequence or a punishment. When you met that first cop, you likely instantly knew when you saw the flashing lights in your mirror that you had made a choice that was going to cost you. You had prior knowledge that disregarding stop signs would cause tickets with fines and points, so you were prepared to accept that consequence, though unhappily. What choice did you have? Argue with the cop about the law? But the first cop took the consequence of your action and added a little of his own punishment (anger, sarcasm, humiliation, fear), which caused you to focus only upon his anger, not your driving issue. And your thoughts then were mostly about wanting to strike back, not about driving safely. Consequences must be administered without hurtfulness or they become punishments. That second cop was all about punishment-free consequences intended to teach, not hurt.

Good parental consequences are constructed prior to a first offense, when we're calm and thoughtful, and usually in the light of day. These are our best work and our hardest, especially after our kid does something for which we were not prepared (such as, well, almost everything?). A price we pay for teaching for the future versus hurting for the moment is not being able to administer a consequence for a first offense that has not been discussed in advance (unless the behavior is imminently life-threatening—see Part III). This father, Anthony, found out how difficult that can be, as he tried really, really hard to shake off his prior training:

"This consequence versus punishment stuff is 180 degrees from what my Italian father would have done. Makes me feel like a fish out of water. Three weeks ago, my 14-year-old son came home drunk at 1:30 in the morning and I did what [members of his parenting group] have been training to do. I took some deep breaths until I could push back my anger and quietly said, 'I know you've been drinking and we'll talk tomorrow about that. Tonight I'll stay up to watch while you sleep to be sure you don't stop breathing or inhale your vomit, which can kill you.' My son just looked ashamed. I think that's good!

"As I sat up watching him, fighting my urge to slap him around, I was reading our notes [about what to do in this situation]. I suddenly remembered my coming home drunk at 16 and my own father screaming and cursing and slapping me in front of my younger sisters. They were crying. I remember hating him and wanting to get back at him so bad. People say 'hate' is an overused word, but that's what I remember feeling. I was really sorry that I had been drinking, but only because it kept me from being able to kick the sh-t out of him. I remembered that for a long while after that night, I did everything I could to hurt my father, including drinking more.

"When my son woke up the next morning, I made him a coffee and then I asked him, 'What did you learn?' He just stared at the floor, real uncomfortable. I think he wanted me to hit him like I used to. I get now how that would have really just let him off the hook. Then he could just hate me for hurting him and not think about what he had done. So I showed him some research I found about what alcohol does to teenagers and told him this stuff scares the hell out of me because I love him. Then I set up the consequence of what would happen if he does this again and asked him to think about all of this. He never said a word.

"The truth is I still don't know how I feel about handling it that way. Actually, I do. My {C} brain feels unsatisfied, like I wasn't a real man or something. My {P} brain is calling me a bad parent, and weak. I guess that's my old man stuck in my head, right? My {A} brain? My {A} brain says that what I did was pretty damn cool. So I'm OK. My son? For three weeks he's been more respectful than he's been in years. What's that about?"

Your second cop can answer that. She knew that using the anger of punishments would not do anything except maybe cause you to drive furiously, perhaps leading to more body parts at intersections. She knew that if she calmly and caringly administered a consequence, it would take your eye off her power and place it exactly where it needed to be: on your unsafe behaviors. Plus, you respected the hell out of her cool, caring, but firm composure. Which cop triggered your {C} brain to simply react emotionally, and which might get your {A} brain to learn rationally? Which cop had the best chance of actually getting you to drive more safely? Which cop do you want to be to your teen?

Last but not least, always use the consequence system to build the resilience life skill of good decision making by linking your teen's level of autonomy with his level of responsibility:

> "I know you want the freedom of away sleepovers," you say, "but I worry bad things can happen there. How about if you earn that privilege by showing me a month of good decision making? After that, you can earn your next away sleepover by doing well with the first one. If you make a poor decision, can we agree that you need a month of no away sleepovers to think and mature a bit before we try again? Is that fair?"
>
> "What?" he yells. "You'll take away my sleepovers if I mess up?"
>
> "No," you respond. "It's all up to you. You'll just earn or fail to earn the month's sleepovers. The power is in your hands to make whatever happens happen. That's the way this world works. Good luck! I'm rooting for you!"

An after-the-fact punishment with no provision of earning back the lost privilege ("You just lost sleepovers forever!") puts a kid on her bed staring at the ceiling like a terrorist with nothing to lose, passionately plotting revenge. A pre-informed consequence is very different: "Sorry. As you know, your bad decision means you haven't earned sleepaways for a month, but I know you'll get the hang of this decision-making stuff. Plan for your next one in four weeks. In the meantime, ask the kids over here" (where, of course, you can supervise things more closely than those other parents). That tactic puts a kid with everything to gain in front of her mirror soberly asking, "Why did I make a choice like that knowing what it could cost me? What the hell is up with me? How can I make sure I earn that privilege back?" Revenge fantasies and actions destroy resilience. Anger at ourselves, really at our own {C} brains, is the start of psychological change and the energy for another step on the journey toward resilience. By the way, when she yells, "But the kids won't come over here" give her a wry smile and ask. "Gee, honey, why is that?"

2. Talk Smart: The Hard Part of Communication

It is no overstatement to say that when it involves teenagers, communication is as essential to resilience-building connection (see Chapter 5) as breathing is to life. If you can't communicate effectively, you have no way of acquiring the critical "nutrients" that allow you to survive and flourish in this world. The scary part is the research showing that our kids learn the bulk of their communication skills from their parents (i.e., us) and from their screens. OMG indeed!

Talking with a teenager is an acquired skill, one counterintuitive to us parents. In "communicating" with our kids, we often fall into that joke/truth about how Americans talk at language-challenged foreigners: loudly, repetitively, and often with dismissive frustration. This tells them we think that they're stupid and not able to think on an advanced level, all because they don't speak our language well. My multilingual friends (whose skills make me feel stupid) tell me that American English is the hardest popular language to learn due to its complexity and illogical constructs.

With our kids, the problem is that when they were very young they were sort of stupid and not able to think on an advanced level. But just like those tourists, when kids grow into adolescence they are much smarter creatures with much smarter thoughts, and they are now attempting to master the incredibly complex task of adult discourse. That involves coordinating several different brain regions with breath control and vocal cord tension to create precisely nuanced mouth noises and body language that convey very complex thoughts and emotions. Since you do this amazing trick every day without a thought, you've forgotten how frustrating it was for you as a young teen. In fact, learning to sing opera is a simpler process for adolescents than learning to give voice to their emotions. They often feel like foreigners cast adrift in a mysterious world that can isolate them in a kind of "Man in the Iron Mask" verbal prison, where their thought capabilities far outrun their ability to vocalize them. That's a tough place to be. Ask Ross:

> When my son wasn't yet a year old, he was a delightfully stupid bubbling mass of nonsense sounds with an occasional almost-word randomly thrown in. We were driving past a farm when he started bobbing in his car seat and loudly and excitedly saying, "Damses, damses."
>
> "Yeah," my wife and I flatly responded, "dances." We assumed he was simply miming my brother talking about the dance concerts he promoted at that time.
>
> *"No!"* Ross yelled. *"Damses! Damses!"* His frustration only grew as we continued to imply his stupidity based upon his poor vocalization skills by returning the affirming and corrective response of "Dances." (You can see we were highly educated parents.)
>
> He was red-faced and upset when with great exasperation he finally exposed our arrogance and our ignorance: *"Damses!*

Damses! You know, baaaah!" Cindy and I stared at each other in astonishment as we pulled over to look at the "damses"—an incredible miracle of beautiful lambs frolicking in a gorgeous pasture that our wise son was mindful enough to truly appreciate, and caring enough to try and share with his highly educated, self-absorbed parents.

If that story touches your heart, save that empathy for your teenager since she's going through exactly that same process where she holds complex and powerful thoughts and feelings that have temporarily outraced the brain wiring required to express them well. So speak carefully, following a set of respectful rules you'd follow if you were talking with a language-impaired stroke victim, knowing that their bungled words are a terrible estimation of their clear and stressed minds. Here are some effective parent-to-teen speaking rules:

- **Be aware of timing.** Sleep-deprived mornings are lousy times for serious teen conversations and, for many teens, not a time for any conversations. After school might be even worse since they're sick of adult criticism from teachers and coaches. Psychologist and author Mike Riera says if you want a good conversation with your teen, set your alarm clock for midnight. He's referring to the fact that when the world is going to sleep, teenagers' brains want to stay awake. They get so desperate for human interaction they'll even talk to you.

- **Be alert to quantity.** Less is definitely more. After your seventh word, many teens begin hearing Charlie Brown's "Whaaa, whaaa, whaaa . . ." Choose your words carefully.

■ **Take care with volume.** *The Smoker You Drink, the Player You Get* is the mysterious title of Joe Walsh's 1973 album, which he refused to interpret. However, I recently figured it out. He was advising parents about the fact that the louder we talk, the less teens hear. Yelling, demeaning, forceful speech simply fires up their {C} brain. Save your breath until you can be less "smoker."

■ **Speak questions, not answers.** Your resilience-building goal in talking with your kid is talking as little as possible and listening as much as possible. Remember your mission of helping her learn to control herself? That comes from her thinking about her own actions, values, and beliefs, a process that ends once we being lecturing them with answers as we see them. Instead of "Here's what you should do," try "What do you think you should do?" Their thinking and talking in response to good questions gets those deficient brain wires exercising and getting stronger right before your eyes, building resilience.

■ **Observe the fences.** There should always be a boundary in conversation where we stay on our side of the fence when speaking as much as possible. Climbing over the fence into your neighbor's yard or your teen's business to tell him what's wrong with him ("You know what your problem is?") might not work out so well. Instead, observe the boundary with your teen and try "I" statements: "When you come home late, I get angry because I'm scared."

■ **Dose carefully.** Some of the best teen conversations are not a single marathon but 10 sprints. Remember how trying this process can be for your teen and watch the horizon of her face for the storm clouds of exhaustion and frustration. When those appear, consider them as rumblings of thunder, warnings that the storm is not far behind: "Hey, I appreciate you hanging in on this talk. How about we take a break and chat more later on?"

■ **Retreat when storms strike.** If you pressed too far and he blows up, run the hell away. Many parents (mostly dads) hate when I say this, but nothing good and a lot bad can happen once the raging starts. Even and especially if your teen is verbally abusive, just disengage. First calmly offer one chance at continuing: "If you want me to stay and talk, please stop the insults." But if that fails, get out of Dodge. If you do what might come naturally and scream back, you're trying to put out a fire with gasoline. Good luck with that. Part III will give you the full rage response training you need to reduce the odds of lightening striking twice.

3. Listen Smarter: The Harder Part of Communication

Why is it that we parents just can't shut up? Is that really so hard to do? There's a great Looney Tunes cartoon I love/hate where an adolescent bird tries desperately to get a word in edgewise as his self-appointed mentor, Foghorn Leghorn, runs on endlessly about everything that's wrong with his small protégé. "But . . . but . . . but," the poor chick tries to explain. Foghorn feels disrespected: "If y'all don't quit flappin' ya jaws, son, how ya evah gonna heeah MAH point of view?" It makes me laugh every time I see it probably because it's too close to home for me.

The reason you and I can't shut up is because we love our kids and get in such a control-freak rush to fix their problems that we cut them off and verbally run over them. We might as well shut up since no one is really listening. Besides saving energy and frustration, our shutting up turns out to be perhaps the key part of great connection/resilience-building conversations for a couple of reasons.

First, skilled listening can provide a hole in time and space for your kid to fill with words, giving both of you some insight into her thoughts and feelings, and starting the process of improving both of those things.

Second, it can convey a healing sense of caring because you are simply listening without judging, advising, or defending, especially when your kid is saying things you don't want to hear. The world is overflowing with people who seem so eager to judge and tell him what to do. The gold for your kid is finding someone who listens caringly, which means pushing back our own need to fix (i.e., control) our kid and pushing forward our willingness to listen to and care about what he thinks, especially when we disagree. That stuff is resilience gold since he learns to organize and convey his thoughts in a connected relationship that often involves disagreement. Skilled listening does not mean that you agree with his thoughts or necessarily give your approval for him to act them out. It just shows that you value and respect his thinking.

In Part III, we will talk about what to do when communication with your kid seems nonexistent, but here are a few listening tips to help you with your kid:

- **Don't interrupt.** Allow 10 seconds after she stops talking and ask for more if she has any: "Thanks for sharing that. Is there more you'd like to add?"

- **Do the empathy trick.** Empathy is not sympathy. Empathy is listening to someone not to see *if what they say makes sense to you,* but to see *how what they say makes sense to them.* That can be a little rough at times:

Angela was the poster woman for the overprotective moms' association. She was deeply religious and told me that she preached to her 15-year-old adopted daughter, Marianna, many times about postponing sex for marriage. Alone in the first session, Angela told me that she didn't think she could ever tolerate the thought of her daughter being "promiscu ous" by having unmarried sex. When they came in for a joint session a few weeks later, Marianna looked like she was facing a firing squad. "Mom," she stammered, "I, I know this will kill you but, well, I've been talking this over with Dr. Bradley, and, well, I decided there's something that I need to tell you about. For, like, the past two years, I've been, you know, like having, you know, sex with a boy."

Mother and daughter each took sharp breaths. "The truth is," Marianna said to her shoes, "with a few boys." Tears hit them both at the same time. "Please don't hate me, Mom!" she pleaded. "I heard all you said and I really wanted to be that way but there's something wrong inside me. Dr. Bradley asked me to think of what I'm doing as a symptom, not a sin, and try to understand it. I think it has to do with being adopted. There's like this black hole in me where I can't feel loved, although you and Dad do everything great for me, but it just hasn't filled in that hole. It's like I need love and acceptance that I try to get from sex with boys but that makes me feel worse, so then I do the same dumb thing over and over, feeling worse and worse." Marianna was crying hard now. "I guess there's no way you could ever forgive me now. I understand if you want me to leave the house since I'm like just this horrible slut."

The silence was so absolute that the only thing heard was sniffling for a minute that felt like an hour. I was so scared for Angela's reaction that I had a hard time looking at her. She slowly got up, and Marianna's crying exploded into sobbing, thinking her adoptive mother was leaving her just as her birth mother had. But Angela rushed to where Marianna was sitting on the couch, knelt next to her, and held her fast and hard while Marianna sobbed in her arms.

Angela had just taken a huge step in building connection and resilience with her wounded daughter, and in building her resilience Angela had been listening. With empathy.

—From the author's personal journal

■ **Advise only if invited.** Wait until he's clearly done talking before you advise or comment (unless it's an emergency—see Part III), and then do so only with his permission to climb over that fence into his business:

> "Wow, son. That's sounds painful. Thanks for sharing that. Would you like to know my thoughts?"
>
> "No, Dad, I don't. No disrespect but I feel like I need to figure this out on my own. Is that OK?"
>
> "Absolutely, son. I'm always here if you change your mind."

■ **Change the venue.** If chatting doesn't seem to happen at home, try the coffee shop or even cruising around town. It's amazing how differently kids interact in different places.

■ **See "Student Communicator" written on his forehead.** When teens are learning to drive, a "Student Driver" sign placed on the rear bumper can inspire a lot of forgiveness and patience from otherwise angry drivers frustrated at the learner's slow pace and poor skills. Similarly, give your teen a lot of space and patience when he's talking. Don't take what he says literally, and be extremely forgiving of his "accidents." He will "hate" you at times when he really means that he's upset with you. He will start out yelling about something insane *("I can't believe you forgot my Oreos!")* and often transition into the real pain if you use the verbal judo of a deflecting, non-challenging response:

> "Sorry about that. I know how you love them. So, how's the rest of your world doing?"
>
> "Well, it sucks! I'm not nearly as important to you as my 'perfect' sister! You never forget her stuff! Nobody ever cares about what's important to me. Not you, not Dad, and not my girlfriend who thinks I should have a car like Derek, that creep who's hitting on her and probably will get her to break up with me . . ."

■ **Ding! You just heard what the Oreos were really about.**

Teens often say too little and shout too much, but the shouting can be another form of communication. Become tough enough to withstand non-abusive yelling and wait it out without interrupting and yelling back. If you can hang on, your kid often becomes calmer and says what really has her upset. Her anger might not be about your forbidding her drug use, but more about losing friends who use if she doesn't. If we're patient with student driver/communicators, they eventually do become skilled at both things. And they also love us more for cutting them slack when they were awful at both.

4. Keep Selling, Especially When They Ain't Buying

Staying connected through the dark days of adolescence, those times when they want to be no closer than 10 linear feet, is easier said than done. Getting some precious hugging and conversation can feel like finding water in the desert. But both are precious to life, so never quit trying. Even when your kid responds to your "how about a hug?" request as if it's a bizarre sexual fetish by snarling, *"Gaaawd, Mom. Pleeeze stop asking that!"* don't do as he requests. Instead, try: "OK. I get that at 14 you're too old for that huggy stuff. But I've always got a hug waiting here for you."

Believe it or not, your kid gets sad when you accept his own words that he's too old for that huggy stuff. Remember that those arrogant 14-year-olds are largely 4-year-olds in big bodies with bigger stresses that are wearing them down terribly. Hugs help, *even when they're refused,* and are amazing builders of resilience. Just the offer reminds and reassures them that you are still there to catch them when they fall, as they are bound to do. Knowing that we have spotters in our worlds is a huge part of resilience.

So be that great salesperson and refuse to take no for an answer when it comes to connections with your kid. Here are two tips for when things are really, really bad. I wish I could take credit for them, but these are from two of the best saleswomen moms I ever met:

"Dr. Bradley, tonight when you were talking [in a seminar] about somehow staying connected to our kids, I thought of something I did that helped when my daughter had not spoken to me for four days no matter what I said. I can't even remember why she was so mad. If you think it's OK, maybe you could put this idea in one of your books. On that fourth day, I couldn't stand it anymore. I don't know if it was divine providence or my crazy Greek brain, but this idea just came to me. I filled two water pistols, put them on a silver tray, and presented them to my daughter. 'Choose your weapon,' I said in this Terminator kind of voice. She looked at the pistols and said, 'You're a stupid psycho-mom. Get the hell out of my room.'

"'OK,' I answered. And I picked up a gun and started to shoot her in the head! With water, of course. She was screaming, *'You're nuts! You're a whack job! Stop! Dad! Get Mom out of my room! She's berserko attacking me!'*

"My husband is a smart Greek man. He knows to stay out of a fight between two Greek women. I wouldn't let up. She finally picked up the other gun and started shooting back. The next thing I knew, we were chasing each other through the house in front of the astonished males, screaming and shooting and soaking each other, and laughing hysterically. *And remembering that we loved each other.*"

If water guns aren't your thing, another mom offered another tactic that teenage males might find even more violent:

"When my son turned 13, it was like some 'get away from me' switch flipped in his head. After hearing you [in a parenting seminar] explain that because of sexual development, boys can get weird for a while about physical contact with parents, I get it now. But I felt terribly distant from my kid and I knew he was going through tough times, and I needed to break that ice somehow. Tell me if this was a mistake. His friends were over and he was acting his old surly self with me again, so bad that even one of his friends told him to lighten up with me, but that made him even angrier.

"So I went up to my room and rummaged through my closet, not really knowing what I was looking for. An answer, maybe? I found an old, really gaudy sombrero from an unfortunate trip to Tijuana back in the day, and some crazy, iridescent purple lipstick from an old Halloween getup. I put on the sombrero and about two pounds of the lipstick and went downstairs and crept up behind my son, signaling his friends to hush. Their eyes got huge. I looked like a cartoon! When my son caught on and turned, he literally screamed like when he was three! I started to chase him around the room growling, *'Give Mummy a kish! Give Mummy a kish!'* When I cornered him on the couch, he finally began laughing like I haven't heard for a year. It was wonderful.

"Since then when I ask for a hug he usually smiles and says, 'OK! OK! But no lipstick, right?'"

Giving up any pride and self-respect you might have left turns out to be amazingly empowering when it comes to reaching out to connect with a teen.

5. Think "Resilience" in All Parenting Decisions and Discussions: It's Not About Tonight—*It's About Forever*

The easy part of this tactic is always looking to hand power to your teens so they can make every possible (non–life-threatening) decision completely on their own. The older they get, the dumber we should act (this comes naturally to me): "Son, I really don't know if having purple hair will upset your sister when we take her wedding pictures. I guess you need to decide." This serves two goals. First, it helps your teen feel more of the autonomy his brain desperately craves, as it should. Remember this is his "re-birthing" time, morphing into an independent human being. The second goal relates to the first one, namely that he needs to build his decision-making skills to survive. And sadly for us, the only way that happens is for teens to practice making decisions, not have us do that for them.

Remember that parental decision-making mantra: *The bad decision made well teaches far more than the good decision made poorly.* The good one made poorly is the one we take out of their hands and make for them. That teaches them how smart we are and that they should delegate decisions to us forever. The bad one made well is where we love them enough to step back and let them do something dumb (but not life-threatening), watch them get punched in the face (metaphorically), dust them off, and softly ask, "What did you learn?" And then we love them enough to comment only if they want.

The hard part of this tactic is trying to break that terrible, resilience-crushing habit of reflexively making the most efficient (controlling) response and instead think about the resilience-building (teaching to control) one. My trick is always delaying any response so I can think a bit. That can be hard. For example, when your daughter asks to go to the pot party in the park, do not instantly yell, "Are you insane?" You already know that you're never giving your permission, so use the questions you ask as windows of opportunity get her to begin to develop her own values. You've already discovered that randomly preaching at her about something like drug or alcohol use rarely gets through her lecture deflector shields. But she has to lower those shields when she starts those conversations. Try asking, "Do you think it's OK for 15-year-olds to smoke weed?" When she says yes, ask for her science: "Who says it's OK?"

She may then give you the "Everyone does it and half my friends' parents are OK with it" line. To which you reply, "I'm sure that's true. When I was a kid, many of my friends and their parents said cigarettes couldn't hurt you. What else tells you it's OK?"

"In Europe, kids smoke when they're like 14 and they learn how to use weed safely," she says. "Really?" you answer. "Well, let's both do a little research on the science of what weed does to teen brains and meet later tonight to share what we find."

Why add so much time and trouble to such simple issues? Because when they ask for your approval for things such as drugs or sex or quitting school, their {A} brains are open for learning critical things that will eventually shape their life values and resilience. Yelling "No!" shuts down the {A} brain that might have looked at your research and thought, "Wow! Weed might cause permanent brain damage." Your "No!" flips on the power switch to their {C} brains that say, "We'll see who wins this one."

6. Be Cool with Not Being Cool: In Adolescence, "Hate" Is the New "Love"

Remember in Chapter 4 when we spoke about the 10-point continuum of parenting and of how the sweet spots were at the 4, 5, or 6 positions? Well, those sweet spots can be a little sour when the payoff for your efforts is hearing how much you are hated. But your {A} brain should interpret that as being *loved*:

Becky was all in on this one. She stood over her seated mom to emphasize her words: *"All of the other parents are cool with this! Why can't you be cool with this?"* At 14, Becky was in a terrible bind. Eight of her friends had somehow gotten parental permission to travel to Cancun on an unsupervised, coed spring break trip, to which Becky's mother, Linda, was "insanely" opposed. The group ranged in age from 14 to 18. As Becky paused her yelling for a bit, I studied Linda's weary face, which was lined at least a decade beyond her 50 years. Over the past year, her husband had left without warning to live with a 25-year-old, taking with him their three older boys, who wanted to live with their "party" father who would let them do whatever. At 14, Becky could choose to live with whichever parent she wished. She had opted to stay with Linda. I circled that as "interesting" on my history notes.

Becky had reloaded and was ready for a second go: *"Dad already gave me the check, so it won't even cost you a frickin' penny! He says I can go if you say OK."* Linda's eyes locked with mine. I sighed and nodded softly, signaling that I saw how Becky's dad had set Linda up to lose her last child. Right on cue, Becky yelled, *"If you don't let me go, I'll—I'll—I'll move in with Dad and I'll never talk to you again!"* And then (proving my theory about how much smarter teen girls are than their male peers), she hissed a quiet, razor-sharp threat through gritted teeth: *"And you will never, ever see my children!"*

I wanted to ask Becky for her autograph since she was such a great psychological sniper: It was as if she was thinking, "OK, size up my target. What's Mom's greatest vulnerability? I got it! Loss of family, loss of children! Threaten her with losing me, her last child, and her future grandchildren. That should do it."

Her shot found its mark. Linda's exhausted eyes filled with tears as she looked to me to somehow fix this. I gave her the "shrink shrug," wordlessly saying, "Sorry, but this has to be your stand. If I could fix this, I shouldn't." Linda likely wondered why she was paying all this money for me to simply shrug, but she had no time to argue about that. Her daughter's life was hanging in the balance. She took a deep breath, turned back to her daughter, and showed what she was made of. And she showed it perfectly:

"Becky, I love you. I love you way too much to let you go on that trip. Terrible things happen on these trips. Maybe there's some other fun we could plan. I know this breaks your heart but I'm older and smarter than you. I love you too much to let you do something dangerous because you threaten to leave me. That would hurt me terribly but my happiness is not important here. It's all about what's best for you. Sorry, but my answer is no."

Becky leapt to her feet wide-eyed. She tried to tower over the glass-topped coffee table that separated her from Linda and screamed that fire-alarm scream only 14-year-old girls can scream. *"I hate you! I'll hate you forever! Aaaiiiieeeee . . ."* and she kicked over the coffee table. The glass shattered as she ran out of the office still shrieking, slamming my office door so hard the wall clock fell onto the floor. She ran out into the darkness of the parking lot, still screaming, but then strategically stopped running so that we could still see and hear her. The other docs started opening their suite doors to see what was up, but they turned around when they saw it was just another "Doc Mike" moment.

Linda started to cry. "See, Dr. Bradley," she sobbed, "I'm losing my last child."

"No, you're not," I softly corrected. "You're gaining that child. Look, Becky's just crazy, she's not stupid. She gets it.

She knows her father set you up, and she knows this trip is a really bad idea. She also knows that you love her enough to say no, and to then sit there and take that raft of crap she just unloaded on you. Why do you think she chose to stay with you when she could live with her party dad? She knows she's safer with you, that she's not ready to solo in the world, that she still very much needs her mom. She's a banana out in the parking lot because she knows all of that smart stuff *and* she just really, really, really wants to go to Cancun. Wouldn't you at 14, even knowing it was a bad idea?"

Parenting a teen is a relationship based on love and conflict. It's your job to "ruin" her life at times, and it's her job to "hate" you at least as often. In the proper dose, rage-free conflict with parents can be very therapeutic for kids and builds heaps of resilience by teaching them how people can disagree passionately and still remain loving and connected. Always bookend your difficult messages to your teen with love: "We love you. Terrible things can happen at that beer party you want to go to. We love you too much to allow that. Sorry."

Don't think that the "business" of parenting will ruin the "personal" of caring. It won't, unless your {C} brain gets provoked into attacking your kid personally in retaliation for her attacking you. Keeping your {A} brain focused on the issue at hand gives her the best chance of doing the same and perhaps learning something. Remember that on the scale of parenting, the 1 and 10 feel like a lack of caring. The 4, 5, and 6 feel like love to teenagers, even when they're raging bananas in Dr. Bradley's parking lot. And speaking of raging bananas . . .

7. Narrate Your Anger, Don't Become It: There's No Teen Problem Your Rage Can't Make Worse

When parents ask me to identify the single most effective tactic for changing our teenagers, I answer "Changing ourselves." And the single most effective self-change we can make is to manage our own emotions in full view of our kids so they can watch and start to learn that trick—which is actually very hard to do. Remember in Chapter 4 when we talked about how apology is a Trojan horse of life lessons? So is modeling. For better or worse, our children are more influenced by watching us parents than by any other of the formidable powers in their worlds. Scary, isn't it? But perhaps it is also hopeful. For it is a way we can safely and secretly shape them a bit without a war. Remember, the bottom line is that ultimately we really cannot force our teens do anything they flat-out refuse to do. And angrily punishing their defiance with our power leads us down that dictator's path of creating rebels with nothing to lose:

Miguel looked so incredibly sad. "Thanks for coming," he mumbled to the floor. "My dad, he won't, you know, come to visit me now. He said he's teaching me a lesson for my own good. I don't know . . ." I had not seen this 16-year-old boy in more than two years, but I instantly recalled his once sweet, caring nature, now concealed by a gunfighter's face. "Since we saw you, things just got worse and worse. My padre, he's a tough man, you know? A good man but a hard man. I always wanted to be as tough as him, you know? Never take no sh-t from nobody, never back down, you know? I wanted him to look at me one day and say, 'There's my son. He's even tougher than me!' I wanted that so bad, and now, it's like, I don't know

. . . I just lost it when he called me 'chavala.' That means like what you call being a pussy."

Two years earlier, Miguel's father had stormed out of our last therapy session yelling about my "weak-ass bullsh-t" conflict resolution advice: "Some 'wedo' [white guy] tells me to not get in my son's face? What would you know about where we come from? He's got to learn to be tough. You tell me don't get in my son's face when he disobeys and disrespects me? OK, and then one day he goes to prison 'cause he has no respect."

I was visiting Miguel in prison. He was sent there after assaulting and seriously injuring his father. His father had been "teaching" his son about toughness and respect by daring Miguel to punch him while he shoved and slapped Miguel repeatedly for forgetting his chores. His father was right about one thing. His method did make his boy tough. Miguel had won the fight.

Miguel's Hispanic father and my own Irish one were both brutal *and good* men trapped by very bad ideas. They believed good parents use rage to toughen and teach children to become what we would call resilient. That was their version of love. Try not to judge these men harshly since in their world, the bad parent would not care what their kid did, would not get in their face. They thought that becoming their rage was an act of love for their kids. And a lot of us parents still do. The big secret in America is that most parents hit their kids, often well into adolescence. Some states use laws to protect parents and thus promote beating children (they call it "corporal punishment") even though endless and massive research always proves that, at best, it's a waste of time.[1] At worst, it ends with guys like me visiting once sweet kids like Miguel in prison.

"Whoa! Wait one minute, Dr. Bradley!" you yell. "My father, my football coach, and my drill sergeant all slapped me around, and I turned out OK. And from what I'm reading, so did yours! And you turned out OK, right?" This challenge is thrown at me at about half of the parenting seminars I do. I usually take the Fifth Amendment regarding if I turned out OK, but I always ask my challenger the following: "Sir, please tell me about your own father." The challengers' responses are always almost identical: "Well, my father worked two terrible jobs to get us all through school, he coached everything, and he still somehow found the time to take care of the fatherless kids down the street. The man never owned a decent pair of pants or shoes. He just gave it all away."

"What a wonderful story," I answer. "Sir, you just told me about your father's values and character, things that overwhelmed you with love, admiration, and respect for the man. You never mentioned the hitting. You *forgave or overlooked* the hitting because you *admired* the man. You are likely a good father today *not* because he became his anger, but rather from how you saw your father live his life."

Parental modeling can be a curse or a blessing. It all depends upon what we are modeling. If we allow ourselves to snap out over our frustrations about missed chores or bad grades, how can we expect our kids to not freak out over their own frustrations? Conversely, if we calmly narrate our anger instead of becoming it, we have then earned the right to ask them to do the same. Getting that kind of control requires some martial arts training.

EMOTIONAL JUDO FOR EGO STATES

When you find the month-old nacho leftovers moving slowly out from under your kid's bed (conveyed by the happiest and smallest of God's creatures) and you want to explode on your teen (a true Dr. Bradley vignette), try some judo—on yourself, not your kid. Judo is about using leverage and balance to control and deflect negative energy. When I saw the aged nachos (I'll spare you what else the creatures were celebrating), it was very late after an exhausting and conflict-ridden teen day. My {C} brain immediately flew into a rage and transformed my entire body (remember that it's the brain that grabs control of our physical state). Thanks to the {C}'s adrenaline rush, my blood pressure and heart and respiration rates all soared. Boundless energy was directed toward my collective speech processes to enable a great scream. For a nanosecond, I even pictured slapping my kid and feeling very satisfied. Then my judo training kicked in. "Never fight mad," my Army martial arts instructor taught me. (I hadn't realized at the time that he was a student of Eric Berne.) So I did the judo steps:

1. Do nothing and freeze in place.

2. Take three very deep breaths and exhale each slowly.

3. Use my now accessible {A} brain to ask my {C} brain what my real pain is, since anger is usually a second emotion triggered by a preceding one:

   {A} "Why do you feel like exploding on your kid?"
   {C} *"I'm furious!"*

   {A} "Because?"
   {C} *"Her room is a pigsty!"*

{A} "So?"

{C} *"She never does what I ask."*

{A} "So?"

{C} *"That shows she doesn't respect me!"*

{A} "So?"

{C} *"That shows she doesn't care about me!"*

{A} "So?"

{C} *"I think that's it. I want to hurt her because she doesn't care about me. I feel hurt and uncared for."*

{A} "OK. I can see why you feel so bad. You go chill out. I'll take care of this."

Having clicked the firing safety back on my {C} brain, I confront my kid, narrating what's in my {C} brain but not becoming it: "Sarah, when I find food under your bed after you've promised not to do that, it makes me feel like you don't care about me or what we need to keep the house well. As crazy as it might sound, it feels really crummy and makes me want to scream and yell. Can we agree that if it happens again, you're telling us both you are not ready for the privilege of having food in your room? Does that work?"

Here's that other resilience parenting mantra once again: *Be what you want to see.* When it comes to anger, model *narrating* it, not *becoming* it. That means no hitting, threatening, or belittling. Ever. Hurting teens to teach them to not be hurtful teaches only that might (physical or verbal) makes right. What can feel very powerful to your {C} brain can look very weak to your kid and cost you dearly in respect currency. Worse, the real issues (such as drugs or sex) get buried in the cage match of a power contest. Getting hurtful with a teenager is playing in her stadium—you're giving her the home field advantage of suggesting that rage is a way of "solving" problems. Remember that she is willing to get crazier than you. Don't go there.

"TOO LATE, DR. B . . ."

So now that you've already gone there and lost it by screaming and shouting and maybe even slapping, don't despair. Welcome to the club! Many parents get despondent reading parenting books that set parental behavior goals that seem unattainable. That's because perfection is unattainable, even for those of us smug enough to write parenting books. I believe that our failures are part of the grand design of effective resilience parenting, that our imperfections are placed there by God, Mother Nature, or whomever, to provide great excuses for teaching resilience skills to our kids.

We've spoken about how apology is a magnificent teaching tool for things such as owning our behaviors, wrestling with imperfection, and striving to do better. Well, here you go! Your screwup moment can be a grow-up moment for your kid through the magic of apology. Teens are nothing if not imperfect, so they learn a lot and are comforted by seeing adults who freely admit to their own shortcomings as shortcomings, never justifying their loss of control as somehow acceptable simply because they're parents. Wrong is wrong.

We don't have to be perfect, and likely shouldn't be. We do have to be honest.

8. Encourage Identity Explorations

*"The two most important days in your life are the day
you are born and the day you find out why."*
—Mark Twain

Another point of near universal agreement among experts in adolescence is the absolute criticalness of identity development in teenagers (remember, the brain development clock runs to at least 25 years). Beyond all else, this must be a time of figuring out who the heck they are and how they safely and happily fit into this often bizarre and always potentially overwhelming carnival called existence. Once that identity thing happens, you can almost hear the "click" that goes off inside their heads and suddenly they look different.

Think of everything of worth to a human being and ultimately you are talking about identity. That includes higher-level values and beliefs (e.g., "It's not about me," per Pastor Rick Warren) and codes of conduct and realistic self-insight and acceptance. When you hear that "click," get out of the way because passion, purpose, and real achievement fall quickly into place, and your job is pretty much done. Sound good? It is incredible. And getting there can be hell on parents. Take this case involving 19-year-old Jarret, who was sitting in the room with his head down:

"Dr. Bradley," Jarret's mother said, "Jarret tells us he wants to drop out of college and play video games. He did really well in his first year at college in a hard engineering program. We think he's having some sort of breakdown or something."

Jarret lifted his head. "Really, Mom? Is that what you heard me say?"

As Jarret turned to address me, I had a hunch he should address his mother and stepfather instead. "Jarret, please just direct your thoughts to them," I said. "I'm not the one who really needs to hear you."

He got it and turned back to them. "Look," he began, "first, I'm incredibly grateful for all you guys have done for me. This is not about rejecting you or engineering or anything else." He paused. "It's—it's hard to explain. Engineering is OK, but I don't feel alive doing that stuff. I know this will sound like I'm a spoiled brat, but, well, when I play my game I'm like transformed. I feel incredibly alive. I don't think you guys get this since you hate video games. They're not what you think. I gave you that binder to read, the one you threw away, to help you understand. My 'game' is now a multi-billion-dollar business with sponsored teams and pros who make their livings playing this. My scores are just below pro level and I only practice two hours a day. I might be great at this! But I'm not stupid. I know the odds are huge that if I take this year and take a shot, I'll be headed back to school next fall. But I won't be tortured by this thought in my head that maybe, just maybe, I could have been a pro."

He turned to his stepfather: "Pop, you've told me like 10 times about how when you were 18, you decided to leave home to try to make your living as a poet in Haight-Ashbury, and your parents went nuts, and you nearly starved to death. And you always tell me how amazing that failure was for you, that you learned so much about the world and yourself, and that you don't regret a minute of that, since it helped you become the good man you are."

Jarret turned to his mother: "Dad [his biological father] never did anything like that, remember? He was always so serious and practical. He always bragged about how hard he worked from when he was, like, seven years old to become a radiologist. How the hell does anyone know at seven that they want to or should be a radiologist? He never let me do anything he thought was a 'waste of valuable time' [said with finger quotes and a deep voice]. Then one night when he was like 50, he never comes home, and he begins running around with girls just a little older than me. And he still is. He says it's his 'midlife crisis.' Something's really wrong with that phrase. I don't know why I'm talking about Dad, but it's connected somehow."

Jarret paused, as everyone in the room seemed to be in deep thought based on the ramblings of this "crazy" 19-year-old. I decided to break the silence. I turned to his parents and asked, "If Jarret said he wanted to take a year off from school to try to pitch for the New York Yankees, how would you be with that?"

As Jarret was speaking, my mind had flashed back to a get-together my friends and I had held in a bar for Ricky, our high school hero and baseball pitcher friend who everyone had known would dominate the major leagues one day. After all, he had been signed by a pro team right out of high school. After graduation, we each went our separate ways, hearing sporadically about Ricky working his way up the arduous and unglamorous minor league steps toward the majors. Finally, after hearing that Ricky was hanging up his cleats after what we saw as wasted years pursuing his stupid dream, we held a sad reunion in a bar that we once frequented.

"What's up with you guys?" Ricky asked. "You're acting like we're at a funeral or something."

"Ricky," I said, "we feel really bad for you. We all kind of were able to do things that we wanted to do like school and the military and such, while you, you know, you . . ." My voice trailed off.

Ricky pushed back his chair and pointed to the old guys at the end of the bar. "You see those old guys? The woulda-shoulda-coulda guys, always talking about what they wished they had done when they were young? I'm never going to be one of them. Look, guys, I chased my dream. I gave it all I had. I got to try out in *New York Yankee Freakin' Stadium*! I wasn't good enough. I got crushed. And that's OK. I'm headed for some new adventure now, don't know what exactly yet, but I know I'll be OK because I'm not afraid to work hard and chase my dreams. I just know I'm gonna succeed."

Forty years ago, Ricky's words in that smoke-filled bar were another of those rare lightning bolt moments for me: *It's is not about winning the game. It's about playing the game with everything you've got!* Forty years later, I now know that Ricky had built his core identity while "wasting" all those years chasing his "stupid" dream. He was resilient. He later became successful doing crazy high-risk construction projects around the world. When praised at a later gathering as this incredible all-time winner, he again stunned us: "All-time winner?" he laughed. "Forty percent of the time I crash and burn. I'm always one step away from going from millionaire to welfare. My success is based on my 10 percent edge, and that's it. And I could lose that tomorrow!" As he easily laughed at his own financial fragility, that old lightning bolt flashed again, this time with a few new words: *Resilience-based happiness is not about winning the game. It's about playing the game with everything you've got!*

I hate to depress you more than you might be already, but nobody wins this game of life in the way that we parents like to pretend for our children. Nobody lives forever. It's not about safely playing the cards of elite schools, sports training camps, and summer enrichment programs, as entitled folks like to believe will bring happiness to their kids. The less entitled should know that college alone is by no means the guarantor of life happiness for your kid. *It's about how they will use the time they have here.* And to become wise enough to figure that out, they need to figure out who the heck they are, to develop their identities. And to do that, while they are still young, they need to chase "stupid" dreams a bit and to have parents wise enough to know when it is time to step back and hand control over to them to "waste" time chasing rainbows.

9. Buy Them Off

> *"Never underestimate the effectiveness*
> *of a straight cash bribe."*
> —Journalist Claud Cockburn

OK. I've put this off long enough. Here's where the psychologist readers stop reading and start typing angry book reviews and snarky letters to me. We're about to enter the bribery wars of teen motivation.

First, know that I plead guilty to saying "bribery" versus "incentive" as a provocation intended to get people thinking by stirring pots. My past critics have accurately pointed out that "bribing" connotes paying people to do unethical or immoral things, something we should never do with children. They beg me to instead use the word "incentivizing." I would but it's easier to pronounce "bribing." Besides, I think readers are smart enough to know that we're really talking about the serious debate concerning whether kids should get material rewards for doing what we think is good for them (i.e., extrinsic motivation).

Stated oversimply, the anti-bribers believe that kids should do the right thing for its own sake and the internal payoff of doing the right thing (i.e., intrinsic motivation). I say, "Great! I agree! But what do we do when the kid in question doesn't care about those intrinsic payoffs?" The anti-bribers suggest then trying harder for that intrinsic motivation. But for how long and at what cost? For example, there could be lost reading skills, the lost resilience-building achievement components required for competence and confidence, or the habituation of achievement-avoidant behaviors into negative identity (e.g., "I'm stupid and lazy").

I believe research proves fairly conclusively that this debate should not be oversimplified to intrinsic versus extrinsic motivation. Rather, the debate should be about figuring out which system works best for which kid and when. Everyone agrees that intrinsic motivation should be the ultimate goal for all kids, but in case you haven't yet noticed, teens from the same family gene pool can be radically different in many profound ways, one of which is innate motivational systems and levels of maturity at certain ages. Parenting wouldn't provide as much fun/terror if our kids were all the same, right? Some are easily intrinsically motivated and some are not. So when your son Moe bitterly complains that his younger brother Curly gets paid for doing homework, your answer is, "Sorry, but when you were 13 you were dumb enough to just do your homework." Or said more positively, "At 13 you were so wonderfully mature that you knew how important homework is. Curly needs a little help for now. But your great example will help him a lot. Thank you for that."

Most experts suggest trying the intrinsic route first. That means holding off on the bribes and instead offering affirmative feedback acknowledging real effort, not empty praise and platitudes: "I was very impressed with how hard you worked at that science project. How do you feel about that?" Failing that, then consider offering the straight cash bribes of money or earned privileges.

Another reason I believe in teen bribery is how well it builds upon the resilience-focused discipline system we discussed earlier in this chapter, in Tactic #1. The well-designed consequences we discussed focus upon responding to negative teen behaviors in ways that encourage resilience-building decision-making growth. But how can you encourage other resilience-building activities that your kid seems determined to avoid? Bribe (or "incentivize") them!

Think for a moment about your own life. What got you to try difficult, challenging, growth-producing things? I'm sure sometimes you were intrinsically motivated to take on some challenge, but always? I'll also bet there were times you were shooting for some extrinsic payoff when taking a risk. And perhaps that all helped to build your resilience. It surely did for this kid:

When I was barely 16, I desperately needed a job since my family was poor and my dad had lost his job. I really wanted money. I had gotten my driver's license a week before when I saw a job listing go up on the school bulletin board: "Wanted: Stock and delivery boy for Rosa's Pharmacy. Must have driver's license and be able to drive a manual transmission."

Of course, being a good Catholic boy, I stole the posting off the board and called as soon as school let out. Carmen Rosa answered the phone. After we chatted a bit, he said, "Sounds as if you're a good candidate but I've spoken to other good kids as well. Whoever gets here first today will get the job." I was panicked. I had no idea how to drive a stick. My best friend then was Mario D'Alfonso. (He was 110 percent Italian, but the Irish versus Italian wars were winding down in 11th grade.) He was a rich kid driving a beautiful orange MGB with, of course, a stick shift. He gave me both a ride to the pharmacy and a crash (pun intended) 15-minute course on driving a stick. I was awful but Mario said, "You won't have to drive today, right? We can practice more before you have to drive their car." That calmed me a lot.

I got there first! The interview went great. Carmen asked about driving stick shift and I, of course, being a good Catholic boy, lied: "Oh, yeah," I bragged. "Been driving stick all my life."

Carmen's eyes suddenly twinkled for some reason at this barely 16-year-old boy. "OK," he said, "just one more thing. Take the VW out on the Pike [a very busy four-lane highway in front of the store] so I can see how good you are with the stick. Drive down a few blocks, do a U-turn, come back and park, and the job is yours."

My stomach knotted with panic. I could barely drive, let alone with a stick, let alone on a busy highway. Being Irish helped, though. It has to do with believing in magic. I thought, "Hey, you did drive some stick coming here. How hard can it be?" So I climbed into the VW, found first gear, and pulled out into traffic. Now to those unfamiliar with the nuanced differences between a 1967 MGB (a sports car) and a 1966 Volkswagen Beetle (not at all a sports car), the glaring one would be the shifter. In the MGB the shifting distance between the gears might have been two inches. In the VW, I discovered, those distances were measured in feet. No Irish magic could save me now. I was able to somehow find second gear and stayed there, feigning excessive caution due to the traffic. "Hey," I thought, "I can stay in second the whole time and maybe pull this off." And so I did. Almost.

On the return trip, traffic cursedly died for a bit so I had to drive at normal highway speed. In second gear, the engine was dangerously maxed out at about 25 mph, and I knew this was not looking or sounding good. As I approached the store, there in front stood Carmen and Mario, two South Philly "Goombahs" (slang for Italians), chatting away while evaluating my NASCAR skills. Being directly in front of them, I decided it was now or never, they could only hang me once, so I went for third gear. I missed it by only about a foot and a half and instead somehow jammed it into first (adrenaline is amazing stuff) and let out the clutch.

It is hard to describe the sounds that occurred. The Beetle decelerated from 25 mph to about 1 mph in half a second. The rear tires were screeching, shuddering, and smoking, and the engine and transmission were screaming like dying Transformers. Drivers behind me were violently swerving on both sides of the shrieking Beetle, blaring their horns, screaming and throwing fingers. Miraculously, there was no crash. I limped the gasping, smoldering Beetle back into Carmen's parking lot, not being able to even look at him, wondering how much this repair was going to cost me. I had tears in my eyes and found it difficult to unhinge my fingers from the steering wheel. Then I heard this even stranger noise. Laughter!

Carmen and Mario were both staggering over to the still-smoking car, doubled over in hysteria, slapping each other on the back, pointing at me, looking at each other, and then roaring with more laughter. Carmen also had tears in his eyes, but of a different sort. As he wiped them, with great difficulty he laughed out the following words: "You dumb-ass Mick! Anybody who needs this job that bad, well, he deserves it! Go home and let your Goombah friend here teach you how to drive a stick. You can practice on the VW tomorrow." I still couldn't quite get this. "You mean, I mean, you're saying . . . ?" They both were laughing again. "Yes!" Carmen bellowed, waving his hands and laughing with his trademarked mock accent, *"You gotta' 'da job!"*

—From the author's personal journal

I share that humiliating but true story to paint the picture of how much or most of this resilience stuff actually occurs. First, know that it was strictly an extrinsic "bribe" (the prospect of a job and salary) that got me to stare down all of my 16-year-old "dumb-ass Mick" fears. That job was the beginning of a transformative, resilience-building relationship with Carmen that changed my life. Second, the entire experience occurred out of my parents' sight. Parents would like to think that resilience happens in soft, safe, calm experiences such as volunteering at the food bank, and that's partially true. But a lot of it happens in fits and starts that are anything but soft, safe, and calm. Unfortunately, a lot of parenting books promote those soft illusions, and that causes parents to panic when their kid does crazy things such as lying about driving a stick shift. As you saw in Tactic #8, much of the best resilience growth occurs amid conflict, risk, and stress, all of which are therapeutic in the proper dose. But that chaos puts a lot of us off, and so we stifle our kids by being too controlling.

So first, take a look at your own control needs before you start to think about messing with your kid. If she seems to be stepping up and embracing challenge and appropriate risk, even to a point that makes you uncomfortable, then forget the bribes and get out of her way. You may love her honors courses and sports tryouts while hating her playing weird music in a scary-looking band. Or you may hate her wanting to take a gap year while loving her plans to build freshwater systems in Africa. All of those out-of-your-control love/hate things mean you've got a kid who is intrinsically motivated. Congratulations!

But how do you motivate the teen who seems to want to do nothing? The "effectiveness of a straight cash bribe" (to quote Claud Cockburn) or incentive can often get that kid over the hump of his inertia or anxiety or lack of belief in himself to take a shot at something that can have a huge payoff in helping him learn to not let his {C} brain talk him out of trying anything worthwhile. When it comes to the science of building resilience in troubled teens, success indeed builds success. This means that one simple growth experience enables the next by increasing the skills, beliefs, and brain wiring that make previously "impossible" tasks suddenly appear within reach. Foster those baby steps in the beginning and soon you'll see leaps and bounds happening on their own. With some luck, he might even blow up a Volkswagen.

The final trick with bribes is using them to get kids to employ healthy habits that they might otherwise never try. In Part III, we'll flesh out some specific examples such as getting more sleep, stopping the use of weed, and maybe even eating something green and not fried. Bribes can do all of that.

"But Dr. Bradley," you protest, "I was just at a lecture and the shrink there said if you pay your kid to do something healthy, he'll stop when you stop paying him." Well, maybe, but maybe not. The trick is that if the kid won't do the healthy thing for intrinsic reasons, the money gets him to experience the healthy behavior. Over time, those behaviors that were initially extrinsically motivated—such as getting paid for getting enough sleep— produce secondary intrinsic payoffs. For example, enough sleep can create payoffs such as feeling better physically, getting compliments from suddenly smiling teachers about classroom performance, getting kudos from happy coaches about better batting averages, and even seeing less acne in the mirror. All those payoffs can make those extrinsically inspired behaviors become lifelong identity features. Even if he quits the behavior, he quits after having had that positive experience that he might well draw on in the future when the unhealthiness gets too painful. Bribes can be a no-lose resilience tactic.

So go ahead and bribe your kid as you need to, but please don't tell anyone I said so. (I get enough hate mail as it is.) Claud Cockburn also said: "Believe nothing until it has been officially denied." OK. So for the record, I never said bribing could help build resilience.

10. Love Your Partner—Especially When You Hate Each Other

You might be puzzled to see this tactic on a list of teen resilience-building tricks but it turns out that one of the best resilience gifts you can give to your teen is to love and respect her other parent. Children are to their parents' relationship what planets are to the sun. When that core relationship is solid and healthy, the planets are all held safely in place, using that positive energy as both a reference point and a model. That same type of stable reference point has helped teens from forever handle their radical developmental changes.

Kids can change so much so fast that their heads spin worse than their parents'. This can be very unsettling to teens, as if terra firma itself becomes periodically questionable and unreliable. For contemporary adolescents in this electronic age, that disorienting effect of "OK, *now* what is real?" can be exponentially worse as their entire worlds can shift at the push of a "send" button. This can shove them toward warping out into the dark regions of space. Having extremely boring, maddeningly consistent, perfectly predictable, and mutually loving parents becomes a wonderful lighthouse, a cheery, resilience-building beacon of light for teens adrift in the stormy and often threatening seas of adolescence. Even though they'll hate it at times:

My son was well into his dark phase of becoming a rock star at 13, trying to write songs about everything uplifting in the world, including death, dying, social injustice, war, poverty, misery, hopelessness, corruption, and on and on. Simultaneously and wordlessly, he seemed to suddenly hold my wife and me in utter distaste, as if we stood for everything he despised. "I guess he thinks we're just a couple of sellouts," I quipped to my wife.

One night, with his black guitar slung around his black-shirted shoulder, he confronted us as we sat on the couch, holding hands and laughing at a movie. "Why'd you have to raise me in this stupid town? Nothing bad ever happens around here. Why do you guys have to be so boring? All my friends' parents cheat, fight, get drunk, and are divorced!" As he stormed off, he yelled, "*I wish we lived in* [and he named a crime-ridden part of Philadelphia]. *I've got nothing to write about!*" I was tempted to call after him, offering to get drunk, throw the empties on the floor, sell some crack, and beat him to a pulp, but he likely didn't think I was "real" enough to do any of that.

—From the author's personal journal

The modeling part of your partner relationship is presented to your kid when she unknowingly observes and takes in the day-to-day art of good relationships which, like ice dancing, can appear so effortless and seamless and yet is the end product of hard work and boundless selflessness and mutual support. Her first few boyfriends will likely make you think I was nuts to say that, but just wait. I'll bet her "forever" life-partner choice will have an eerie resemblance to her boring old man.

IF YOU PARENTS ARE TOGETHER . . .

. . . use that "ice dancing" discipline of remembering that something that exquisite requires constant practice and team-building. Here are a few exercises:

■ **Do the 10,000 kindnesses.** I apologize profusely to the person who long ago invented this concept, which moved me so much I forgot her/his name (and Google has forgotten her/him as well). Always look for small ways to remind your partner that they are number one in your life and that you've always got their back. Things that work well include love notes on wind shields, silly dollar gifts, and out-of-the-blue hugs given with words such as "Thanks for being here with me." We all need the affirmation, and never more than when things get tough with our teens.

■ **In your "family business" world, support your partner (almost) unconditionally.** Short of allowing terrible verbal or physical assaults, always support your partner's calls—their decisions on the business of parenting your teen. Disagree later if you must, out of earshot of your kid, but do so remembering what a crazy hard business this teen parenting stuff can be. It's often about difficult decisions made under fire by exhausted parents, calls that often have no clear right or wrong answers. Monday morning quarterbacks who judge and criticize their partners often find themselves playing the next game alone. Partners who without judgment acknowledge the difficulty of parenting often stay together forever. Know also that the teenage strategy of "divide and conquer the parents" comes naturally. Be like two cops in a bad neighborhood in the middle of the night. They know that nothing good will happen if they do not support each other, so when they confront a tough situation, it's shoulder to shoulder. Their disagreements occur out of sight. Together as one they are much more formidable than as two apart. That can calm things down quick.

■ **In your personal world, date (each other, that is).** Remember dates? I mean the real ones, like before you were dumb enough to have kids? They were personal, not business. Back then you didn't go to dinner to debate curfews, drug tests, or SAT prep courses. You just hung out together, right? You would just ask your partner, "How are you?" and when she said, "Fine," you'd say, "No, really, *how are you*?" And then you'd sit and listen, just feeling privileged to be part of her world. Re-create that magic and watch how calming that can be for a stressed teen.

IF YOU PARENTS ARE APART . . .

. . . building a good working relationship becomes even more important. Before you yell at me because you despise your ex (whom you may have good reason to despise), think for a minute. You and your ex are not finished your tour of duty quite yet. Your personal partnership is over but the business one (the children) need more skilled and disciplined parenting by the two of you than ever before. The fact that you may not like each other has nothing to do with how your kids feel about the two of you. Remember that, like it or not, a kid's parents have more modeling impact upon them than any other force in their worlds, and that includes separated partners. The odds are great that your teen loves and respects you both and needs you to be at least respectful of each other. He also needs you to be able to work as an effective team in any interactions that fall upon him. Hearing one parent he loves denigrate the other he loves creates a toxin that may cause him to physically and emotionally retreat from both parents, since it's just too painful to hear them say awful things about each other.

Ironically, teens may unconsciously bait one parent into talking trash about the other as a kind of test to see (and learn) how people can have serious conflicts and yet maintain a dignified human respect for the other, never attacking the person but simply disagreeing on the issue. Before you eagerly go for that bait your kid might set out, which could perfectly align with your own separate anger toward your ex, remember Benjamin Franklin's words as paraphrased by Marvin Gaye: "Believe half of what you see, son, and none of what you hear."

If your kid's trash talk about your ex is just a test for you, you will flunk if you pile on. And if your kid's words have some truth, you'll still flunk if you pile on. Better to say, "Wow! I can see you're really mad at Mom. I can't answer for her, and it's unfair for me to take sides without her being here, so perhaps you should talk this through with her. Maybe see a counselor together if you can't work it out. I know she loves you and wants what's best for you even though you disagree." Restrain your own anger from falling out on your kid. Love him enough to show respect for his other parent no matter how difficult that might be for you personally. If it helps, know that in his heart, your kid will carry your grades on those tests for the rest of his life.

Together or apart, if you have serious concerns about how your partner or ex interacts with your teen, suggest that as a family you all sit down with a counselor to see how each of you can do things better.

11. Make a Joke

I know I started out this section by promising "10 Terrific Tactics" and not 11. But do you know how hard it is to alliterate 11?

That was a joke. Think for a moment about what it did to your internal process. Perhaps it broke your often burdensome parental chain of heavy thought and emotions, especially the ones that come with parenting teenagers. Perhaps some of the funny stories shared in this book did the same. Did that irrelevant silliness sort of refresh your brain a bit, like restarting a slow computer, perhaps knocking down your concern or anxiety levels a tad and allowing you to calm a bit and suddenly see other perspectives? That is exactly the magic of humor, the last ditch defense against fear for cops in squad cars, soldiers in foxholes, and parents of contemporary adolescents.

This tactic is a critical tool in building your kid's resilience by always trying to take nothing too seriously, including your kid's behaviors, her attitudes, and most important, your own reactions to those things. If you can find the humor in the darkness, it can light up your soul:

My 17-year-old daughter and I had a terrible standoff the other night. Sarah was demanding to go down the shore for an unsupervised weekend with her friends. When we finally said "Sorry, but no," she went nuts, screaming and yelling to try to bait us into a fight to get what she wanted. One of our resilience goals for her is to learn to tolerate frustration, so this was important on a number of levels. But she's great at the games of rugby and parent provocation and had me pretty much nose-to-nose with her on the steps. She retreated to higher ground (the upper steps) to get the tactical advantage. After exhausting any compromise options, I did the trained response saying, "I'm sorry but the answer is no, and I'm not going to get into a fight with you over this." She put her face an inch from mine and yelled, *"That's because you're a pussy!"*

The range of emotions and thoughts that flashed inside me in a nanosecond was striking. My {A} brain was very impressed that she somehow intuited and manipulated my tendency to overreact to aggression, a leftover scar from my being bullied as a kid. A second was my {C} brain urge to prove to her that I was not a pussy by doing—*what, exactly?* Getting as insane as her? Maybe screaming back, *"I am not a pussy!"*

My final reaction was my salvation. Laughter! This was all just too funny! "Yep," I affirmed to her. "I'm afraid you're not the first person to ever tell me that." Ever since that night, my daughter's insult has become a sanity-saving, go-to joke between my wife and me.

—From the author's personal journal

Learning to never take anything too seriously—including our kids' crazy behaviors, our world, and especially ourselves—is an amazing skill to model for our teens as a great resilience remedy for stress and fear. Even dark humor is better than staying stuck in the hopelessness. Laughing at scary things gives us a desperately needed sense of some control over chaos. Tactically, it is also a great response to our kids' rage. After I agreed with Sarah's assessment of my manhood, she turned and stormed away, screaming with the frustration of a rugby player discovering that punching a marshmallow is not very satisfying. I once had a pilot tell me that parenting teens is much like flying jets. He said that it's often not the problems that cause crashes but our impulsive *reactions* to problems that cause catastrophes. So using humor is a great way to build our kids' resilience as well as helping us to safely land imperiled teenagers.

Speaking of safely landing imperiled adolescents who are frequently flying on one engine, you are now finally ready for Part III. In military parlance, you've mastered the basics: the mission, strategies, and tactics. Congratulations! You're now ready for your advanced training. Turn to Part III to see how this all comes together in dealing with the specific resilience and stress challenges you are likely to encounter.

PART III

Common Resilience Parenting Challenges: The DOs and DON'Ts

*"Before I got married I had six theories about raising chil-
dren; now, I have six children and no theories."*
—Poet John Wilmot, Earl of Rochester

I love that quote. Beyond his prescient words, Wilmot's birth/
death dates—he was born in 1647 and died in 1680—reveal an
additional child raising insight for us 21st century parents. The
first is the timelessness of the challenge in raising children (he
writes like a 17th century blogger on parenting woes), particularly concerning their confounding uniqueness, which defeats
our attempts to come up with one parenting paradigm that works
for every teenager. To remedy that problem, Parts I and II have
given you the base knowledge you need to tailor your own set of
resilience-building, stress-reducing responses fitted to your
unique teenager. Now you're ready to see how those things come
together in handling a few of the common teen challenges you're
likely to face. These particular ones were chosen in light of their
uniquely critical impact upon adolescent resilience and stress.

They are also the issues that most frequently drive parents into the offices of teen experts.

These Part III topics are presented as four groupings: behavior issues (acting out, drug use, sleep problems, electronics challenges, stress); school issues (hating school, refusing to work); sex and dating issues (controlling/abusive partners, sexual activity); and social issues (bullying, excessive shyness).

The responses are laid out as what to do ("DO") and what not to do (DON'T) prompts followed by explanations. The DOs and DON'Ts will come in handy at 2 AM if/when one of these problems occurs. These outlines are also easy to get into your long-term memory circuits. But don't just read the lists of DOs. Remember the pilot's advice on flying/parenting (at the end of Chapter 6) about not reacting poorly to problems and crashing. The lists of DON'Ts can keep you from turning manageable crises into catastrophes.

I suggest you review all of these topics for two reasons. First, they will guide you if/when these particular situations occur. Second, since the core concepts in each topic are universal, they will give you frameworks you need to create your own responses to the hundreds of other similar resilience and stress challenges you will face. It will help if you keep those brain ego states—{P}-{A}-{C}—and resilience-building strategies in mind as an overlay as you read. You'll then see how these tactics operationalize those concepts. The rationales following the DOs and DON'Ts spell it all out.

Disclaimers: Be aware that none of these discussions are exhaustive. Each topic is a book in itself (as you'll see in the further reading recommendations in the Appendix). In addition, serious worries are always best addressed with the guidance of a skilled

Licensed Mental Health Professional (LMHP) who is proficient in those particular teen issues.

Oh, I almost forgot. There's another parenting insight I take from John Wilmot's life dates: his early death at the age of 33. One account holds that he drank himself to death.

Did I mention that he had six children?

SEVEN

Behavior Issues

"Teenagers: You can't live with 'em, and you can't kill 'em."

—Kathleen, parent of three teens

Parenting children up to adolescence is much like the regular season in baseball—you know, that relaxed, mostly boring, and seemingly endless time when we often leave the games early to get some ice cream, not knowing the score. "Who cares?" we yawn. "One game doesn't mean much." In the regular season of parenting (up to adolescence), there are always a few heartbreaking losses and some exhilarating wins, but mostly it's a laid-back time in the parenting game. But parenting teenagers is like the playoffs in baseball: You can be on the edge of your seat for every pitch. You know that one bad move can end your entire season in a heartbeat. With teens, one thoughtless word can cause an explosion.

It's another one of Mother Nature's great practical jokes. We get lulled to sleep raising kids from birth to age 11 or 12. It can be hard for a few of us, but relatively speaking, it's easy. We're faster, stronger, and smarter than our kids, and they actually still think that we're sort of cool. They look up to us and mostly do what we ask. And when they don't, we can pick them up and stick them in their rooms for a time-out. Savor those times if you still have them.

If you haven't yet been to those parenting playoffs (adolescence), beware the cosmic karma trap that awaits. Karma can present as a moment when things are going just great with your perfect 10-year-old girl, and you look out your window to see your neighbor on her front lawn being cursed and shrieked at by her 13-year-old daughter. You smugly smile and quietly chortle to yourself, "I'll never let *my* daughter talk to me like that. That mom must have done a bad parenting job."

Don't go there! Parent karma is a real force in the cosmos. Years later, those judgments can come back as old memories to cruelly taunt us for our earlier arrogance as we hear our "perfect" daughter, now 13 herself, cursing and shrieking at us. I can guarantee that any veteran neighbor won't judge you in return. She'll just sadly shake her head or light a candle or say a prayer for you because she's been to the teen behavior wars and knows how tough they can get.

So how do the wars start? Often it's as if some switch flips in their heads. It can be a "Fort Sumter" moment, an astounding first shot across the walls of your perfect relationship. It can appear in a sudden, serious way such as drug use, sexual activity, or rages. More often it begins with a startling sneer at some simple task request that had gone smoothly for a decade: "Get ready for church? Ha! I'm not going to your stupid church and you can't make me!" That's where a terrible realization suddenly smacks us in the face: "I can't control this creature. She's faster, stronger, and maybe smarter than I am. She doesn't think I'm cool anymore. And I can't pick her up and put her in her room now. What on earth happened?"

What happened is that your little darling is growing up. She's *supposed* to become defiant and challenging to some extent. That's her job as she flexes her independence and starts to build/connect her {A} brain, constructing her own beliefs and values apart from yours. *These are good things that eventually will build her resilience and bring her happiness in life.* But initially, her {A} questioning can present as {C} "in-your-face" rebellion. Your job is to concede that she may be bigger and faster—*but not smarter unless you concede that ultimate power to her.* You must elevate your game for the playoffs so that your advantage is no longer based upon size and speed but on smarts.

Is it possible to manage teen problem behaviors with just our wits? It's not only possible but critical. But before we get smart about our kids, we must first get smart about ourselves by seeing their behavior challenges as simply part of the business side of parenting. *These are not personal attacks on us,* although they can sure feel that way. Much like insurgents, our teens are actually confronting the things we represent, such as authority and control, *but not us as people.* Once you get that view in place, the tactics presented here are a lot easier to use, and they work. Without that mindset, though, there are no tactics that will help.

Keep in mind that your job is about so much more than just managing (controlling) adolescent challenges. While your own parents simply had to control you, the new world requires that you keep your kid safe *while building his resilience.* Comparing your job to that of your parents is like equating the dancing of Ginger Rogers to that of Fred Astaire. Like Ginger, you must dance "backwards and in high heels."[1] These tactics will give you the skills of balance and grace that will get you gliding with your teen just like Ginger did with Fred, even through the times when you want to punch him in the face. I'll bet Ginger had a few of those as well.

Acts Out

Acting out can involve yelling, nagging, provoking, and hurling insults and curses.

Do:

✔ Take deep breaths to stay calm in your {A} brain. He's the amateur; you're the pro. Act like a pro, especially when you don't feel like one. Be silent versus be crazy. A fortune cookie I once got nailed it: "Open brain before open mouth. Foot much harder to stick in brain." Amen brother.

✔ Sidestep provocations. He's just fishing to distract you from the real issue. Don't bite and let him hook your {C} brain. Walk away if you're too angry to keep cool. Nothing good will happen if you stay. Otherwise, you're being controlled by a four-year-old: *your own {C} brain.*

✔ Postpone but affirm. Say, "I get it that it makes you mad that your friends all stay out later than you. We'll discuss this tomorrow unless you can talk calmly now."

✔ Look for a compromise *if* he can calm himself and speak respectfully, and if you can too. Only make decisions from your {A} brain.

✔ Offer one chance for a "mulligan" (a do over) after he says something outrageous: "Do you want to try saying that in a different way?" If he ups the ante with a sneering curse, say OK and walk.

Don't:

✗ Take this personally. If you are, your four-year-old {C} brain is calling your shots.

✗ Get sarcastic or snappy in return. If you do that, you're on her home field.

✗ Start taking away stuff or grounding her on the spot. You can always do that later if need be.

✗ Make decisions while you're angry or frustrated. Instead, say: "I'm too upset to decide now. Check with me in an hour. I'll have your answer then."

✗ Ever give in simply to stop her disrespect or badgering. That's negotiating with a terrorist who just saw how to get what she wants.

All teens experiment with acting out to some degree. It is a critical *and healthy* part of how children develop resilience by learning how to handle conflict productively. The idea is to never do business with her {C} brain or from yours, so that she learns that her best chance of success is using her {A}. Your rage reaction to your teen's acting out will only make it more likely to happen again. Parental yelling, hitting, pleading, or sarcasm are all very reinforcing to an adolescent brain. See how crazy-silly she looks while raging? We grown-ups look 10 times worse, and it can be addicting to your teen's {C} brain to control big adults with little loud words, especially if the adults go nutso in response and become just other out-of-control teenagers. Parental capitulation (e.g., "I don't care anymore. Just go to that stupid party!) is even more addicting. If that tactic works even occasionally to get a kid what she wants, why on earth would she use any other method? It's vital to establish two resilience-critical realities in your kid's head with your actions: (1) that acting crazy will get nothing good from you or anyone else in the world, and (2) that talking respectfully is the only way to definitely get good attention, and possibly increased autonomy.

Control your {C} brain by using your {A} to see those loud conflicts not as horrible failures but as great *resilience teaching* moments. That arrogant adolescent tone is just an alarm bell telling you that it's time to get back to work building your kid's resilience. And stop thinking that your child is the only one who acts out like this. Even if your kid seems worse than most, then congratulations! Parents earn their old age peace of mind by parenting tough kids who have tough problems. Any fool can raise that "perfect kid" whose greatest stress is which elite college to choose. Even with terribly challenging kids, you can best shape their resilience by working on and showing *your own* (such as staying calm when provoked). For better or worse, our children are more shaped by modeling what we parents show them than by any other force in their world.

Be what you want to see. If your kid constantly hooks your {C} (i.e., gets your goat), get some help—for yourself. If you cannot control your own emotions, you're not in shape to deal with a teenager's. If your kid won't quit his provocation game even after you're better at your own game for several weeks, get some help for the whole family. Something else is likely going on.

If your teen ever threatens or carries out any physical aggression (restraining, hitting, destroying valuable property), find the big strength to get small and quietly say, "If you repeat that I will call 911 since as a family we are in dangerous waters." If he repeats the action or threat, make that call. Most cops are great at handling this stuff, and they are not interested in arresting your teen unless he's truly dangerous to himself or others. This makes the very clear statement that once verbal anger explodes into a physical threat, all parenting is done and it's now time to consult the rage experts: cops. The odds are huge you will only have those embarrassing flashing lights in your driveway once. And the message to your teen is well worth that embarrassment. Otherwise, you are conceding that terrorism is an acceptable way of resolving conflict.

Drugs

"Choose life. Choose a job. Choose a career.
Choose a family . . . But why would I want to do a thing
like that? I chose not to choose life. I chose something else.
And the reasons? There are no reasons.
Who needs reasons when you've got heroin?"

—Ewan McGregor as Mark Renton in the film
Trainspotting (1996)

That quote gave me chills the first time I heard it, and it still does. I get to hear that same message whenever I meet a teen addict. Those words nail the horrific essence of addiction, the absolute domination of the addict's "in the moment" {C} brain after winning a death match with the thoughtful {A}. I share that chilling quote to upset you intentionally in case you are ever tempted to become chill with your kids' "soft" drug use of toxins such as marijuana and alcohol. In my work as an addictions specialist, I never met an addict whose first drug use was injecting heroin or smoking meth. Like with alien abductions, I acknowledge the possibility, but almost every true addict I ever met started with soft drugs *in their teen years*.

True addiction and drug dependence are terms that are often misused. Anyone can become physiologically dependent upon drugs, but that is not what most experts define as true addiction. True addiction is when the drug becomes life itself to a person, when the rest of this world fades away into meaninglessness since nothing else can make life worth living. Reread that quote from *Trainspotting*, and you'll see it.

In one month, I once had two living examples that might make the distinction clear. The first was a 17-year-old girl who said, "I was given Percocet [an opioid pain medication] for my back surgery and I want to stop taking them. I *hate* how I feel on them. I hate not being who I am, but every time I try to stop I get real sick and can't even get to school. I hate drugs. I don't even drink. Can you help me get off these pills?" A few weeks later, a 19-year-old boy told me, "My doc put me on oxy [oxycodone, another narcotic pain medication] last year when I broke my leg and now he won't [prescribe] for me anymore without a note from you. You have to help me get more. I can't stop using them or I get sick, and, besides, I friggin' love how I feel on them. Way better than weed, man. It's the bomb." (Well named, I thought.)

That first client, the girl, was *dependent*, not *addicted*. She had tried weed and booze a few times and stopped. Drugs did not own her. That young man was *dependent and addicted*. He reported smoking weed from the age of 14. Drugs were now his master. He reported that his parents were always "laid back" with his use. He said his father was so "chill" he used to smoke with him sometimes, even though this would upset his mother.

As we'll discuss shortly, being cool with *any* adolescent drug use is to be cool with the image of your completely unresilient child one day possibly sticking needles in her arm. And as I have said, alcohol is not only *a* drug, it is *the* drug. *In several ways, it takes more teen lives than any other.* I yell this at you much as I was tempted to do with some parents who came to see me two years too late:

From the "who's gonna start talking?" looks going back and forth between them, I was guessing that this family's "anti-drug" program was more the dad's idea than the mom's. He began: "I was, I am, really worried about all the drugs out there. So two years ago when Colin turned 14, we decided to do like they do in Europe—you know, where they let kids drink and then they don't abuse drugs or alcohol, right? On weekends, we'd let Colin have a couple of friends sleep over and have, you know, a couple of beers. When they started driving, we took their car keys and were really careful about the amounts we'd let them have to teach them how to handle it. We were not negligent about this."

Mom's eyes rolled. Dad noticed. "Anyway, four weekends ago, they suddenly went nuts and took advantage of that privilege. Colin found our duplicate [car] key and they took off at 3 AM on a joyride." Dad paused and wrung his hands. "After the crash, the kids' injuries were relatively minor. But their [blood alcohol levels] were so high they were all taken to the hospital for alcohol poisoning."

Mom couldn't be silent any longer: "The *truth*, Dr. Bradley, is that for two years we were watching these kids, *and our son*, slowly deteriorate in front of our eyes but we wanted to be blind. Grades, sports, activities—everything good all just slowly went away. Looking back, it's obvious they were using more and more and more. But my husband, he kept saying, 'At least they're not doing drugs.' God help me, I believed that nonsense too." She started to cry. "This is not just my husband's fault. It's *our* fault as parents. The thing I can't forgive myself for is knowing that I chose to be blind *because it seemed easier than the fighting we had with him over drugs.*"

As the father had said, the boys' physical injuries were relatively minor. Their emotional ones, however, would likely be severe. The driver of the other car was coming home to her two children after working late in the ER at the same hospital where the kids ended up. She had suffered serious brain damage.

Two months before these parents came to me, I had published a newsletter on research showing how most European cultures that allow teen drinking have *worse* drug problems than in America. I share this tragic story to dramatically illustrate just one horrific way that all drugs are disasters for teens, and to powerfully make the point that alcohol *is* a dangerous drug, at least as dangerous as any of the others. So please note that when I say "drugs," I am referring to a list of substances that includes alcohol, marijuana (including synthetic weed), salts, pills, heroin, cocaine, meth, ecstasy, and hallucinogens (LSD, shrooms).

If you'd like to kill your kids' resilience and create lethal and lifelong stress for them, just be "cool" with their doing drugs. All of these substances share several key characteristics that explain why this is so.

In ego state terms, these drugs shut down the {A} brain and put the {C} on steroids. Remember that the more you use one set of brain circuits, the more neurologically powerful they become. Would you like your 14-year-old to be four forever? The drugs all provide an escape route to avoid resilience-building levels of appropriate stress that need to be handled by that {A} brain to help our kids grow strong. It's as if the drugs are saying: "Scared of getting rejected if you ask that cute girl to the dance? Scared of getting cut if you try out for the swim team? Worried about your bad grades? Light up, young man! I promise you that stress will go up in smoke." The devil's word is solid. The immediate stress goes away, along with any chance of becoming more resilient.

Drugs all cause uniquely devastating damage to teen brains versus adult ones. One example: Teens who begin regular drug use at age 15 have a 650 percent increased risk of addiction compared with someone who waits to adulthood to use.[2]

In addition, they all promote depression and anxiety in several ways. For example, the "tidal waves" they provide of the brain's pleasure neurotransmitter (dopamine) cause teen brains to change in a terrible way. The beautifully vibrant colors of a spectacular spring morning can cause you to stop in awe and say, "My God, what a great day!" But your kid who was doing drugs last night sees the same day only in gray. The wonderful, life-sustaining, simple joys of life no longer provide his brain the reward they do yours. Which one of you finds life worthwhile for its own joy? Which one of you wants to get high tonight?

To most experts, drugs are *all* gateway drugs for teens, *even or especially alcohol and weed*. With each use, they all very slowly but steadily stop providing the same great brain chemical experience they initially gave. Picture a descending roller coaster and you know what I mean. When teenagers get to the point where they use just to try to get back to what used to be normal, they face that life-altering decision: to quit or to graduate to the next drug, and then to the next drug, and then finally to increasing doses of injected heroin until they no longer need to worry about getting high. Or anything else.

Many folks think that resilience-building is mainly for use with anxiety-ridden honors students who would otherwise be heading for Harvard. If that's not your situation, don't despair. The fact is that resilience parenting is even more effective with drug users who could otherwise be headed for prison.

First Uses of Drugs

Do:

✔ Calm yourself if you find she's impaired. Right now, you need to be a physician first, a parent second.

✔ Check your kid's level of intoxication (regardless of the suspected drug used). If her speech and gait are substantially affected, or if you can't arouse her, *get to the hospital now.* Don't guess she's OK.

✔ Multiply her math. If she says "one pill" or "four beers," that might mean four pills or 16 beers.

✔ Monitor her for the next several hours for possible *increasing* drug effects such as labored/irregular breathing, hallucinations, disorientation, or vomiting. If you see any of these, *get to the hospital.* Don't assume that she's just had "a few beers" so she's going to be OK.

✔ Know that teens can recover from drug overdoses (especially alcohol) faster than adults. *You might be seeing only the tip of her drug iceberg.*

✔ Get a substance abuse evaluation if this behavior repeats. Set this as a consequence of the next use (when addressing this first event the next day).

✔ Consider keeping drug tests (breath alcohol analyzer, multi-drug urine screening kits) in the house to avoid guessing if she's poisoned or how much.

✔ *If you're 100 percent sure she's only slightly intoxicated:* Render the "verdict" tonight and the "sentence" tomorrow. Say: *"I can see that you've been drinking/using a drug. We'll talk tomorrow."* If you have any doubts about her safety, get her checked out at the hospital.

Don't:

✘ Go crazy, regardless of how appealing that seems right now.

✘ Try to handle this issue now, when he's high and you're furious.

✘ Leave him unmonitored assuming that he'll "sleep it off." He might never wake up.

✘ Assume that he's only taken the type and amount of drug(s) he admits to.

✘ Wave this off as a rite of passage. That's a trip he might not finish.

The drugs around our kids and our kids' drug behaviors are more dangerous than in years past. One example is that today's teens have more access to more alcohol and can often achieve levels of intoxication that can be a dangerous overdose for an adolescent. A second is that marijuana is not only exponentially stronger than in the past, but that supercharged herb is available in most American high schools, especially gorgeous elite ones.

Adolescents do not have the adult level of impulse control or adult levels of experience to know when to say when (which is a poor deterrent even for many adults). Their soft brains suffer specific, measurable damage even from small amounts of booze and weed. And they tend to get wired for addiction amazingly more easily than adult brains. Yet, thanks to their adolescent metabolisms, the next day these dangerously overdosed kids can look great, showing no signs of the massive hangover that you would have. That amazing teen physiology can take a 14-year-old, alcohol-poisoned drunk and 12 hours later produce a star soccer player who looks great. That blessing turns out to be a curse since this deludes kids into thinking that a .35 blood alcohol level is no big deal (it can kill) and deludes parents into believing that junior just tossed back one or two last night. Keeping drug tests out of sight but ready at hand in every house with an adolescent makes sense given today's teen world.

Drugs appear in most terrible teen stories of physical assault, sexual assault, sexual disease, unintended pregnancies, and suicide. If that's not enough to get your attention, know that the purveyors of booze—too often parents—have killed more teenagers than all the other dealers/pushers *combined*. And it's not just by way of drinking and driving. One way of killing a drunken teenager is to let him sleep it off since he might not wake up.

Some teenagers vomit as they sleep and then choke to death. Those who vomit and survive often inhale their vomit and then develop a particularly nasty form of pneumonia.

In addition, some teenagers have ingested so much alcohol that they stop breathing in the middle of the night. This sometimes occurs if they also took some type of stimulant med (possibly one they stole from their ADHD brother) and it wears off. They do this to be able to drink more and appear more "macho." Even girls now try to appear alcoholically "macho."

I paint these lovely images to shock you out of the insanely common complacency that "some" adolescent drug use is somehow OK, especially if it's "just booze." I am constantly stunned by parents who would rush their kid to the hospital if they learned that he took a handful of pills, but who roll him into bed if he came home incoherently drunk. Both instances warrant a trip to the ER. Might that 2 AM ride be a waste of time? Hopefully, yes—and that makes it a fine use of time since the annoyed ER staff will likely impress upon your kid that he wasn't partying. *He was poisoning.*

To keep your cool at 2 AM, repeat your mission statement 100 times: *to teach him to control himself.* This is high stakes resilience parenting. Screaming and/or smacking her around for barfing purple passions (wine and grape juice) all over your white carpet will do nothing about her next overdose except perhaps to hasten it. You are competing against a skilled enemy, her culture—a world that wants to hurt her—allied with a brain that doesn't work so good. Using fear won't win your fight. Knowledge conveyed with love will, but those are tools better used the next day after your kid wakes up. The idea is to speak only with her {A} brain, and that can occur only when she's sober.

The game is to try to change his beliefs about drugs. So your first utterance tomorrow should not be a list of punishments. Rather, quietly say, "What did you learn?" If he says that he won't do this again and seems believable ("It was stupid and horrible. Kids were fighting, puking, and I just don't get it. It tastes terrible . . ."), set a consequence in place for the *next* event: "I believe that you intend to not do this again. But what if it does happen? Can we agree that would show us both that you're not ready for the freedom of away sleepovers for a while?" Then insist that you each do a Web search on the effects of drugs on adolescents, and then share that research over coffee (you'll need a double espresso). Your focus must be on getting at your kid's *beliefs* about what drugs truly are and what they do. It is not enough to only control his behavior.

If he seems intent on repeating his poisoning, use consequences designed to establish safety fences around him, but not punishments designed to hurt him. Keep those fences in place until his judgment and control improve.

If drug use continues, get help sooner than later. The longer it goes on, the tougher it becomes to treat. And the deadlier it becomes to your kid. Read on.

Chronic Uses of Drugs

Do:

✔ Know that alcohol and marijuana *are gateway drugs* for many teens.

✔ Know that weed *is a drug,* and today's version of weed is much more potent and damaging than your weed from "back in the day."

✔ Know that prescription pills can be as addicting and dangerous as heroin.

✔ Know that teen brains are much more prone to addiction than adult brains.

✔ Know that heavy drug use can distort his thinking to a point where *you must think for him.*

✔ Calmly confront him, saying that his use is out of control and that he must accept immediate help. This time you are telling, not asking.

✔ Get an immediate evaluation at a rehabilitation/ detoxification facility. If none are available and your child is sick/impaired, immediately go to a crisis center or emergency room to be sure that he's physically safe for the time being until you can get to the experts.

If he refuses help and insists on continued use:

✔ Get his car keys, money, and wallet (but *no* wrestling matches).

✔ Confront him *calmly* but *firmly*: "We know that you are using drugs. We love you, and we will take care of you, and you will be OK, but you must do exactly what we say. You will stay in the house for now."

✔ Call a rehab/detox facility for an immediate evaluation.

✔ Go to the nearest ER if your kid is sick/impaired and no help is immediately available.

✔ Call your relatives, his friends, *and* their parents. Say: "Our son has a serious drug problem. If you care about him, please *do not* give him any money under any circumstances."

✔ Search his belongings to determine what additional drugs he might be using.

✔ Watch him 24/7 until you get help, but do not physically restrain him if he bolts.

✔ Consider forced drug treatment or "rehab-by-cop" (see the next section) if all else fails.

Don't:

✗ Yell, cry, lecture, or ask any questions such as *"Why are you doing this?"* or *"Don't you know that this can kill you?"* You are likely only talking to a four-year-old {C} brain.

✗ Threaten her. Don't say things like: *"If you don't stop this you're out of this house."*

✗ Accept any promises that postpone her getting help (e.g., "I swear I'll stop this time if you don't send me to rehab"). Without treatment, the best predictor of her future is her past.

✗ Give her permission to leave the house. Instead, say: "If you leave we will call the police, and then you might be detoxing in a cell. None of us wants that."

✗ Attempt to detox her at home or to just let her sleep it off. She might not wake up.

If you tried the resilience-building/teaching responses a few times and your teen continues to increasingly use, you must now move to control measures where you become your kid's {A} brain, which is being overrun by the drugs. This is not resilience-building time; this is life-saving time because frequent use of *any* drug is a terrible threat to a teenager. Some poisons, such as heroin, can kill them quick. Others, like booze and weed, usually won't destroy them fast but like a lamprey will slowly suck out their life energy until using becomes the only thing they really care about. In one sense, these soft drugs may be the most damaging of all because so many of us adults do them ourselves, and thus we sort of wink at their use by our kids. One-third of alcohol illegally provided to our children is handed to them by their *parents*. One-fourth of these kids report drinking *with their parents or with a friend's parents.*

Most teens who use won't overdose or become addicts, but too many will. There are some factors that increase the odds of addiction (genetics, parental use, peer use), but there is really no way of knowing which kid is "safely" using. The odds of a 14-year-old who regularly smokes weed and/or drinks becoming an addict are about 1 in 10. (Some research suggests 1 in 8 and even worse if there is addiction in the family history.) We parents cannot play Russian roulette with the lives of our children by ignoring their frequent drug use.

Loving drug-involved children means loving them enough to firmly confront them with quiet words, which often lead to their screaming threats: *"If you send me to rehab, I'll hate you forever."* To which we must respond, "That would break my heart. But I love you enough to lose your love if that's what it takes to give you your life."

Many folks believe that forcing kids into drug treatment is ineffective, that teens must truly want to be there to benefit. But the relapse rate for those who volunteer to go to treatment is about the same as it is for those who are forced to go, suggesting that coerced drug treatment works about as well as elective treatment.[3]

So your mission is to get your heavily drug-involved adolescent into treatment *willingly if possible* (since that's less traumatic) but in any way it takes. Your first move is to simply ask: "Son, it's clear that your use is out of control. Are you ready to get help?" Your second move is to assume control by just telling him that this is the way it has to be without issuing any threats. This works more often than you'd think, appealing to his {A} brain that likely knows that he's in terrible danger but is unable to beat back the {C} on his own in the heat of the moment. If his {A} brain is nowhere to be found (a key indicator of addiction) you must become his {A} brain temporarily and force the treatment issue. Many forward-thinking states have recently put laws into place allowing a teen to be forcibly committed into drug treatment (kudos to you guys—those laws save lives). Tragically, many of these states haven't advertised this because the process is expensive for them (shame on you guys—those laws save lives). These procedures vary widely, so aggressively check with your county and state youth authorities to see what's out there. Your elected officials often have staff that can help you. They get these phone calls more often than anyone thinks. If such programs don't exist in your state, know that unless your kid is in immediate danger of dying (e.g., overdosed) it's very difficult/impossible to legally force him into rehab on your own (check with your local authorities). Which brings us to the last-stand-save-your-addict-child option, which is the greatest source of my hate mail. Following an arrest, any juvenile court can mandate treatment for a minor's drug problem. The good news here is that in most states, juvenile records (for kids under 18 years of age) are usually sealed and/or expunged, thus allowing kids to make mistakes, be given help, and hopefully have no permanent record following them for life (no guarantees on that in this electronic age). But that same offense after their 18th birthday can have terrible and permanent repercussions.

So should you turn your kid who is under 18 in to the police for illegal drug use and/or possession ? Take a very long and hard look at your local juvenile justice system to help you decide about that huge risk. Consult with a local juvenile attorney to get their view without hiring them to represent your kid. Once retained, that lawyer's sworn obligation is only to beat the rap, not get your child treatment. If your local system seems more about helping kids than hurting them, give it some thought. Given the excellent cops and courts in my hometown, I'd rat out my heavily drug-involved, treatment-resistant child in a New York minute.

Let me close this scary topic with two suggestions that are key anti-drug, pro-resilience tools whether your kid uses drugs one time or a thousand times. First, parents often ask how much drug use they should permit since "all kids use to some extent." The answer is zero. If you allow two beers, your kid's teen brain will hear "four." If you tolerate four, you just enabled 14 beers. The research says *any* use by teens is dangerous, so stick with zero. But express that not as if you're running a police state, but as a loving, clear, and firm expectation: "I'm letting you know that it is my expectation that you not use until you are 21."

His likely response? "Dad, that's insane. My friends all use, and half of their parents do, sometimes with us. That just ain't gonna happen."

Then you move closer and lock eyes: "Son, I love you. I'd take a bullet for you. I will do everything I must to keep you from using drugs until you are of age. Please don't test me. I love you way too much to be cool with things that can take you out. I'm afraid that's the thing that 'just ain't gonna happen.'"

Will that kid still use? Likely, yes. But the amazing fact is that a clear, loving, and firm expectation laid out by the parent proves to be a powerful limiter of drug use. We think that's because when his {C} brain says, "Let's go smoke a blunt with Jon and his dad," his {A} brain might answer, "Well, you know, my old man's usually chill about everything. He doesn't get nuts about my grades, or messy room, or even that I dented the car. But he's like berserko on this drug thing. Maybe I should pass on this. Come to think of it, Jon's father does look pretty lame smoking up with kids . . ."

My second suggestion is that you steal my best line (which I've already mentioned in this book) when debating with your teen about the safety of soft drugs such as weed and booze. First, I share the science, which says that every 10th (perhaps every eighth) teen who uses regularly becomes a full-blown addict, a life many see as worse than death.

The smart kids always respond, "That means the odds are 90 percent that I'll be just fine. So, what's the problem?"

To which I answer, "It's like theme park rides. You love roller coasters, right? So if this coaster has this little sign that says, 'WARNING! Every 10th kid who rides loses his life," would you get on? Because that's exactly what you're doing."

Most kids then just stare as if they got punched in the face with a very hard truth. But some sneer, "Sure, I'd still get on." I pause for effect, lock eyes, and in a low voice say, "Then you must really, really freaking love roller coasters *and drugs* to be willing accept a 1 in 10 chance of losing your life on them. Maybe they already own you. Does your response come from your 4-year-old brain or your 14-year-old one? Please don't answer. Please do think. We can talk more later."

Once you are certain that drug use is controlled, her brain is now ready to resume that crucial resilience-building that you must nurture since teen resilience is the best defense against drug abuse.

Obsessive Use of Electronics

"Social media: where men are men, women are women, and kids are predators or cops."
—Ryan, age 13

Do:

✔ Know that his screen (any Internet-accessing device) is your old "corner" (a place to hang out with friends and connect with the world).

✔ Know that some bad but more good happens on "the corner." But the bad can be really, really bad. As in lifelong.

✔ View Internet access like driving: He must prove he's ready to solo via supervised use.

✔ Keep Internet-accessible device use in public or semipublic areas as much as possible (never in the bedroom) until at least age 14.

✔ Link screen autonomy with demonstrated responsibility. Gradually allow privacy in relation to his level of responsibility. Immediately put supervised use back in place if/when the bad happens, but only for a specified length of time. Always work toward their earning autonomy through responsible use.

✔ Monitor to see if his other interests are suffering (sleep, grades, activities, hanging out in person).

✔ Ask him to set a reasonable daily screen time limit and then together review his actual hours after a week without enforcement. Stay quiet as his eyes widen at that number.

✔ If/when his use wildly exceeds his goal, ask him what he can do to cut back his use.

✔ Repeat this monitoring/reviewing drill for a few weeks, again asking him to take charge of the issue while slowly increasing your intrusiveness. Say, "Can we agree that if you are unsuccessful this week, I should just secure your screens at 9 PM? After a month, we can hand them back to see how you do on your own."

✔ Offer rewards for reduced use. Bribe for non-screen time if you must.

✔ Gently raise the point that screen use is flat-out addicting for many kids and can take over their lives just like heroin.

✔ Pull the plug if all else fails, but *only as a last resort*, and simultaneously set up a plan to get him back online but under your use controls until he can begin to self-regulate. If he's unable to get control, get him to a helper (an LMHP).

Don't:

✘ Start out by just pulling the plug (unless you like movies with explosions and teens who can't self-regulate).

✘ Underestimate how important that screen can be to your kid. It feels like her life to her.

✗ Eliminate all computer use to stop the bad. (She'll also miss out on a lot of good.)

✗ Give up and allow her to stay up all night on screens.

✗ Allow totally unsupervised screen access before age 14.

✗ Get into physical confrontations to pull plugs or take screens. Instead, shut off her service/Wi-Fi and/or wait to secure the devices when she's not around.

Like it or not, the Internet has largely replaced the old corner as the place for after-school teen socialization, a function that is critical for adolescent social/emotional development. While many of us contemporary parents wistfully long for the old corner days, our own parents might have opted for the Web for us since terrible teen things happened out in the old real world at least as much as they do online today, and likely more. But there is also a scary downside to the online world, which is likely why you're reading this.

Just like today's parents, parenting experts were mostly caught completely off guard when the screens hit. Few fully anticipated the downsides. The problem wasn't that of child predation, which can occur but hardly ever happens. Your bigger worries are the less dramatic ones that rarely make the news. According to extensive research published by folks such as the American Academy of Pediatrics and the American Academy of Child and Adolescent Psychiatry, these risks include porn addiction and sexual fetishes (now hooking females as well as males); cyberbullying; culture-influenced negative morals, values, and beliefs; weight gain; sleep deprivation; real-world isolation; deficits in social/emotional skills; depression; anxiety; and full-bore screen addiction. These researchers also believe that violent video games can cause desensitization to actual violence (not reacting to it as if it's real) and can actually increase a teen's tendency to engage in the real thing. If these frighteningly common problems sound to you like resilience-killing, stress-promoting toxins, your hearing is good. (Did I mention this is the most stressed generation of teens in 50 years?)

Yet as much as you might hate hearing this, your resilience mission once again is not to simply control screen use but to teach your teen to control her own use since those screens will be with her much longer than you will. Parents using the old mission (control) often just forbid all screen use and thus provide folks like me with a great vacation fund from treating their first-semester college students, who come home crashed and burned after staying up for several nights unable to shut off their suddenly accessible, wildly addictive screens.

A great strategy is to view "screening" exactly as you would driving. Screens and cars are wonderful tools that are essential to your kid's ultimate life happiness. Without careful supervision and training, these things can also maim and kill. You'd never risk your child's life by handing him car keys at age 10 and saying, "Have fun." But that's mostly what we've been doing with screens, and the resulting "crash" numbers are off the charts. Those chickens have come home, but they don't have to roost at your house. Here's how to deal with screens:

■ Never allow completely unsupervised screen use until age 14 at the earliest. That happens to be the expert consensus. My own number is 16. (Maybe I see too many crashes.)

■ Start screen access as late in life as possible. If your kid isn't pleading for a smartphone, stick with that old "dumb" phone till she begs. Some kids actually avoid screens since they've seen bad things happen.

■ When the screen requests become too heartbreaking (it is true that she can become isolated without one), start sharing Web-sourced, teen screen risks with her and ask for her thoughts *without judging or arguing.*

■ Use the driving metaphor, saying you need to be sure she's safe before she solos at 14. Start by installing the parental screen use supervision/control tools. *Do not spy.* Tell her from the start that you will be seeing who/what she says/does, and as you see she is doing well, you will start to pull back those controls until she earns her way to full screen autonomy.

■ Start softly with the least intrusive measures and increase the control only as you need. The idea is for her to learn how to self-regulate. If you just yank the plug (and live to tell the tale), the tale you'll tell is how she only learned how to be offline when you were around and then went screen insane when she left home. The key, as with most everything adolescent, is for her to achieve a workable balance by using her {A} brain to regulate her {C}. That's a trick that will serve as a model for her with other behaviors and a treasure of resilience she'll keep for a lifetime.

Can't or Won't Sleep

Do:

✔ Monitor for signs of sleep deprivation (irritability, agitation, lethargy, napping, poor focus, poor performance).

✔ Take this seriously. (Everything in his life depends upon his sleep.)

✔ Know that he needs nine hours of sleep. That's *per night*, not per week.

✔ Know that he likely gets six or fewer hours on a good night and insists that's all he needs.

✔ Know that his brain pushes his sleep demand into the night. He can push it back with some effort (see below).

✔ Know that he cannot "make it up" or "bank it" for the upcoming week by sleeping all weekend. That pattern actually worsens the problem.

✔ Look for possible related disorders (depression, anxiety, bipolar disorder, sleep disturbances, drug/alcohol use).

✔ Get the screens (TV, computer, phone) out of his bedroom. Bribe if you must.

✔ Get him to try exercising before but not after dinner. (Have I mentioned bribing?)

✔ Research sleep hygiene recommendations online with him.

✔ See a physician if this practice continues. He might have a serious sleep disturbance (sleep apnea, insomnia, restless leg syndrome).

Don't:

✗ Allow TV, phones, or computers in bedrooms (if they're there, bribe them out).

✗ Badger, nag, or yell about sleep. (You'll turn a health issue into a wasting war about power and control.)

✗ Encourage long naps (beyond 20 minutes).

✗ Use any sleeping meds without your doctor's approval. Some can make things worse.

Most folks who work with teens consider lousy sleep habits as the number-one health issue for today's kids, and sleep deprivation happens to be a prime contributor to the resilience loss of this generation. While losing some sleep may not sound very dangerous, it turns out to be a huge factor in teenage epidemic rates of depression, anxiety, car crashes, suicide, obesity, ADHD, type 2 diabetes, and underachievement since exhaustion plays a powerful role in each of those life-altering threats. Sleep is also a very critical time in an adolescent's day when most of her physical growth and development does its thing, and when her brain cleans up its neurological clutter and builds those wires critical to accessing her {A} brain.

Most research says that your kid needs nine to ten hours of sleep a night. I'm ecstatic if my clients get eight hours. Most teens average about six, and that deficit acts like a mismanaged credit card. The nightly shortfall just keeps adding to an overdue balance and gains interest as the week drags on. A kid sleeping two hours less than she needs each night struggles through Monday short two hours. On Tuesday, she's short four hours, and so on. And no, she can't sleep sixteen hours on Saturday and Sunday to pay that off or to bank sleep for the upcoming sleep-deprived week. In fact, those marathon sleeps just make everything worse by blowing up the sleep clock in her brain, a structure that needs to set a regular time to easily zonk out and awaken each day.

A third of our kids stare at their ceilings at midnight because their adolescent brains (on their own) advance their sleep clocks a few hours, so that left alone, they get sleepy at about 1 AM and awaken at noon. Of course, this means that they're near-comatose during chemistry class. Your kid is not lying when she yells, *"I just can't sleep."* What you thought was a desire to party hearty is often just another symptom of adolescent brain rewiring.

Her culture makes the bad worse by surrounding her with addicting screens that destroy her brain's "let's sleep now" chemistry in ways that Starbucks would envy. TVs, computers, pads, and phone screens all stimulate and awaken her brain (even though she swears that TV helps her to sleep). Add in the unprecedented pressures of contemporary adolescent life and you've got a great recipe for chronic exhaustion. I'm amazed that teens function as well (which is poorly) as they do. I'm amazed that some can breathe on Friday mornings.

Your first step is to see if your kid agrees with any of this (which she likely won't) and then see if she'll agree to work to adjust her sleep clock (which she also likely won't). Her exhaustion just feels normal to her, and she probably laughs when you say that she needs nine hours of sleep. Many kids see staying up late as a weird rite of passage, bragging about how late they stayed up the night before the exam/game/prom.

So start by asking her to research this topic on her own and then negotiate (bribe?) for a four-week trial during which she gets more sleep and keeps a daily log noting how she feels. Offering incentives is a neat trick since once you get her sleep clock adjusted forward, her brain will gradually stop staying awake at that new sleep time whether she gets paid or not.

Once she's willing, get the screens out of her environment about an hour prior to the targeted sleep time. "Bedtime" to your kid usually means lying in bed and texting, watching videos, and so on. "Sleep time" means eyes closed, snoring and drooling. This will likely be the toughest part of all for her, so get out your checkbook. If you can afford it, perhaps offer better screens (pads, phones) to be kept outside her room in return for getting rid of the existing ones inside her room. Or simply offer extended privileges and freedoms in return for a more responsible sleep schedule (a great bargain). Warn her that her sleep clock will require patient manipulation to reset, and that she might get frustrated in the process, but that there are tricks that will eventually get it done. She should play with these until she finds the mix that works.

Sleep Hygiene Tricks

- Move bedtime up about 15 minutes each night (from his usual time) until he hits the new target. Do not try to go to sleep three hours earlier in one night.
- Get up at the same time each morning even if he was up late the night before.
- Stop napping or limit naps to 20 minutes. Instead, get up and walk/jog/dance at the old naptime.
- Exercise before (but not after) dinner.
- Turn down the lights in his room, and shut down all screens one hour prior to bedtime.
- Go decaf from noon on. (Realize that chocolate, some sodas, tea, and coffee all have caffeine, which can kill the brain's sleep chemicals.)
- Read prior to sleeping, but on the floor or in a chair, *not in bed.*

- Listen to a soothing white noise machine and/or relaxation tapes/CDs.
- Try earplugs.
- Stick to a nightly sleep ritual (e.g., shower and snack the same time each night before bed). Good sleep snacks include dry unsweetened cereal, pretzels, and turkey.
- Stay calm. Tell him that if he can't sleep well tonight, know that he'll sleep great tomorrow night (if he avoids taking a nap).

Finally, be sure to put sleep into the same priority basket as appearance and messy rooms, meaning that these are things that aren't worth going to war over (where your kid feels that you really hate who she is). Beg and bribe for better sleep, but don't battle. If her sleep becomes a win/lose struggle about who's in charge, sleep deprivation becomes a battle flag in your child's immediate future. Just like learning, sleep is a thing that you cannot force. In time, most kids figure out that they need sleep to do well in the world. And the less we harass them, the more they'll sleep—eventually.

Being Excessively Stressed

"Stress is nothing more than a socially acceptable form of mental illness."
—Author and therapist Richard Carlson (1961–2006)

Do:

✔ Know that this is the most stressed generation of teens we've ever seen.

✔ Know that stress is a mentally and physically ravaging and progressive disease (it gets worse over time).

✔ Know that stress zaps the brain chemistry your teenager needs to cope with his world, which creates a vicious circle by producing more stress that zaps the brain chemistry he needs to . . . and so on.

✔ Listen quietly if he yells non-abusively. Look for themes/clues about his stressors in his ranting.

✔ Model calmness in the face of his craziness. Calm is contagious.

✔ Watch for stress indicators such asfretting, risky behaviors, crying, unusual moodiness, possible drug use, and shifts in sleeping, eating, and social patterns.

✔ Try to help him to improve his diet, get more sleep, try meditation, and get some exercise. These can make *huge* differences. Bribe if you must. By the way, *you first*: Be what you want to see, so improve your own wellness.

✔ Rank order the necessity of his stressors with him and cut the bottom ones, at least temporarily. He may not be able to see his forest of stress for the trees. Ironically, stress can make kids try to do everything, all the time.

✔ Ask if he feels so crummy that he wishes that he wasn't alive. Get an immediate evaluation is he says yes.

✔ See an LMHP if his high stress continues for more than a week or two. Bribe if you must to get him there.

Don't:

. . . .

✗ Underestimate the risks of excessive stress.

✗ Increase her stress by mocking or discounting her feelings. Don't say anything like, "What do you have to be stressed about?"

✗ Give her hollow reassurances like "You'll be fine." It sure doesn't feel that way.

✗ Take charge and make decisions for her unless she's unable to function.

Richard Carlson's is a great one, although a dated one. Today, I believe the mental illness of excessive stress is not only socially acceptable but has now become admirable, signifying hard work, commitment, and effort. In the properly moderate dose, stress is actually a healthy part of an adolescent's development. The appropriate amount of stress resulting from a challenge is a sweet spot for teens where they feel alive, happy, and engaged—a time when they are energized and smiling. In their smiling faces you can actually see their resilience increasing day to day. Creating that smile with the strategies and tactics you've learned is really what this book is about. This section is about what to do when their world dials up that stress beyond their capabilities, where suddenly they're a mess in so many ways and their smiles run away with their wellness. Prolonged overdoses of stress can cripple and even kill an adolescent.

Today's teens are pounded with stressors more than any other generation we've measured. For the successful kids, the "winners," much of the excessive stress comes from increasingly and absurdly demanding academics, bizarre college acceptance competitions, and over-the-top athletics. Many high school sports now "unofficially" demand year-round, excessively time-consuming commitments. The unsuccessful kids, the "losers," are pounded by a ceaseless bombardment of messages of hopelessness that build killer beliefs that they will never be good enough to become a winner. The "winners," the "losers," and everyone in between all suffer from unprecedented stressors coming from a culture that confronts your child with terribly complex social/sexual/drug/violence decisions at ages so young that he has neither the neurology nor the life experience to help him navigate.

Stress overdose is often unrecognized by parents since the ability of teens to tolerate stress can vary a lot. What was fun for your daughter might be agonizing for your son. And the biochemical effects of excessive stress on the brain can lead kids to do screwy, high-risk things to feel better because risk activities create surges in stress-depleted neurotransmitters. This is how that "perfect" kid suddenly finds himself with his pedal to the metal, doing what he knows is crazy and wrong, and feeling terrific for about 10 minutes. Those same biochemical stress effects can also cause his brain to wish that it were no longer alive.

If she goes crazy over her missing Twinkies, don't go crazy in response. She's making no sense because she's really screaming about 10 other things that hurt a lot more than Twinkie withdrawal. Find the grace to love her enough to quietly listen to her rant to see where it goes. As she keeps yelling without your interruption, that lost Twinkie may suddenly morph into her lost best friend, her inability to do chemistry, and five other losses you knew nothing about. View these rants as gifts, as pressure-relief valves that keep teens from blowing apart, and as harmlessly loud words that can help you to see their deadly quiet stressors.

If you know she's stressed out but just suffers in silence, approach her with your concerns but don't insist (badger or nag) that she talk. Say: "I'm worried that you're under a lot of stress. I'd love it if we could talk about that, or perhaps you'd rather chat with a counselor. Please let me know. You really don't have to feel so bad." Teens often have self imposed rules against admitting to being stressed (e.g., it's "weak" to admit it) and try to do the impossible without complaining. Unexpressed stress can overwhelm kids to the point where they'd rather not be alive. Never hesitate to ask her straight-up about that since the more you talk about it, the less likely become the odds of it happening. Say: "Do you ever feel so bad you wish you weren't alive?" If she says yes or is silent (a nonresponse usually means yes), get to an LMHP or crisis center for an urgent risk assessment. If neither is available, consider going to your nearest ER. In any event, get all the guns and potentially lethal pills out of the house. Now.

Don't forget to hug her hard and thank her for telling you, assure her that things will be OK *even though it doesn't feel that way to her,* and say that you are taking over for a bit (becoming her {A}). Then get her the expert help she needs. If she was complaining of crushing chest pain, arm numbness, and shortness of breath, would you guess whether or not she's having a heart attack? So please don't guess on suicide. Some bells can't be un-rung. Once you know she's safe, it's time to dose her heavily on that incredible new stress medication called wellness.

Wellness: The Miraculous Stress Management/Prevention Treatment

"It's not stress that kills us, it is our reaction to it."
—Physician Hans Selye

Hans Selye, who lived from 1907 to 1982, was the first scientist to warn about how excessive stress is a toxin that causes a host of life-threatening conditions, including cardiovascular diseases and cancer. When he first began saying these things, he was pretty much laughed at by his peers, much like your teen might tend to laugh at you. After all, there's no way *feelings* can kick the crap out of your physical being, right? Well, Dr. Selye's peers stopped laughing when they started reading his science. I suspect many also immediately started working less, exercising, eating better, sleeping more, and meditating since these are among the best stress antidotes we possess. Unfortunately, your teen's {A} brain doesn't work as well as those of Dr. S's peers, at least not yet. You likely already know more than enough about wellness (if not, Google it now). What you may not know is how the heck to get your kid to do those wellness things to fight back against the stress that is literally killing his peers exponentially more than it did Dr. S's.

If you get lucky and your kid is welcoming wellness, perhaps you can partner with him to exercise, meditate, and so on. We initially do those things much better with others than alone. But most excessively stressed kids *are too stressed to be able to think well*, let alone find the discipline initially required for wellness. You have to do that stuff for a while before you feel the wonderful benefits that addict you to wellness. So how do you get your excessively stressed kid off that dime if chatting and modeling won't work? Bribe him! Incentivize him with pay and/or privileges to sleep, eat well, exercise, and meditate. As you read in Chapter 6, the bribing will likely only be needed until the wellness addiction kicks in.

In all of the wellness decision making, do as little of the decision making as possible. The more she takes charge of this, the less her efforts will fizzle out after a week, since they'll be *her* efforts, not yours. Remember how "worthless" your parental ideas are to a teenager and you'll have much more influence.

Treatment for Serious Stress Disorders

"The greatest weapon against stress is our ability to choose one thought over another."
—Philosopher and psychologist William James

More than a half-century before Dr. Selye advocated for the amazing power of wellness, William James advocated for the amazing power of *thought* in controlling emotions, writing about concepts that were the predecessors for today's cutting-edge and wonderfully effective anti-stress therapies such as cognitive behavioral therapy (CBT) and dialectical behavioral therapy (DBT). So if your teen is suffering terribly, it's time for immediate CBT or DBT professional treatment to quickly knock down that killer stress to where wellness can manage it forever. In Chapter 3, you read a bit about how those professionally administered treatments work, and work they do! But only if your kid gets there to learn how.

Many teens are very resistant to therapy because of the infuriating cultural bias toward mental illness, but also because the developmental timing for considering treatment sucks. Adolescence is an age when they're supposed to push adults out of their worlds so they become autonomous, and therapy can look like a terrible adult intrusion. That is, until they get there, and then most engage freely and productively.

If your teen refuses, do the wellness-selling drill. First, ask him to consider attending perhaps three sessions to see what it's like before ruling it out. Failing that, go to the bribe: "OK. I hear you saying that therapy is stupid, won't work, and is a waste of your time. How about I put you on salary for therapy?" Many experts just hate this concept, but I offer two thoughts. The first is that your kid's resistance is usually anticipatory fear, and once he gets in the office, that {C} anxiety will begin to diminish and his {A} will start to understand what's happening to him and see how he can help his {C} feel better. The bribe can get him over that fear hump. My second thought is if your treatment-resistant kid is going down the stress drain, isn't offering the bribe better than doing nothing?

EIGHT

School Issues

"They can force me to go to school, but they can't make me learn anything."
—Bumper sticker I saw in my kids' school parking lot

Author's note: Before proceeding, you are required to write the above slogan 100 times. This is mandatory. Spelling and neatness count. Don't forget your margins. Just kidding—you don't have to write anything. But wasn't that annoying, being told what to learn and how to learn it whether you wanted to or not? Didn't you have an immediate {C} brain reaction to resist that order? Imagine how our kids feel. That's pretty much what their school lives are like 24/7.

It's weird how we ex-teenagers forget how awful school can be for adolescents. Not only do we repress those painful memories (such as how agonizingly slow a clock can tick); we also start to build this weird fantasy about how enjoyable school should be for our children. It's often not enjoyable for our children, and as teens they begin to react just like you did a moment ago, becoming annoyed, oppositional, and not wanting to do what they're told. That's when we have one of those painful parent realizations that we can't control our teen the way we wish. These insights wash over us like large waves of astonishment and frustration. And among these waves sometimes comes a tsunami regarding school performance.

That bumper sticker that I quoted perfectly summarizes the dilemma of parents concerning their school-challenged children since forcing a kid to learn is like forcing him to sleep: The more you angrily fight about it, the less he'll sleep—or learn. Using force to accomplish goals like these doesn't work. Economists call such strategies diminishing returns. The more of them you do, the less you get of what you want. In fact, you can get a lot more of what you *don't* want.

Should you helplessly throw up your hands after getting that 10th infuriating note from his teachers? My favorite was the one that implied that I was allowing my kid to screw up school: "Dear Parent: I am very concerned that your son somehow feels it's OK to come to class unenthusiastically and unprepared . . ." There are many things that we can and should do to help our academically ailing adolescents. But like the Serenity Prayer suggests, first decide what you can do and forget about what you can't.

"Hates" School

Do:

✔ Stay calm. More visible parental frustration = less teen school enthusiasm.

✔ View school loathing as a simple maturation issue, not a character flaw.

✔ Agree with his {C} brain that school is boring and mostly irrelevant (it is for most teens). Then . . .

✔ . . . Ask if part of him (his {A} brain) thinks there is any value to school.

✔ Join with the school staff to look for possible undiscovered causes of his hatred of school (e.g., learning challenges, poor sleep/nutrition, disorganization, anxiety, peer influence).

✔ Calmly stay at this. One day he will "get it" if you don't "lose it."

Don't:

✗ Argue that she should love school. You'll only get her more dug in fighting over your power and control, not school.

✗ Just affirm her {C} brain "I hate school" proclamations without calmly tossing in the {A} awakening questions (as noted throughout).

✗ Panic. Many high school haters later discover the relevance and even joy of learning. Let time and the world make your case. Let her chop onions at the diner for 10 hours and then rethink if school is irrelevant to her life. The sky is the limit following that insight.

In the education debates, it is wise to concede certain things from the get-go, such as the fact that school *is* boring and irrelevant—in the minds of most kids. If you're not empathetic with that "school as irrelevant" view, answer quick: What was the gross national product of Yugoslavia in 1980? Was there a Yugoslavia in 1980? *Now* can you recall being forced to memorize dumb stuff you cared nothing about? School is also indisputably the best path to having a good life. The problem is that because of their brain development (as discussed in Chapter 3), teens often find it hard to worry about what might happen decades from now.

If you insist on not conceding that school can be massively boring, then please explain how you compel a 16-year-old to experience rapture in reading *Beowulf*. Did you? Learning for the joy of learning is a typically adult experience that most kids just don't get, and may not get for several years. In the education army, students are mostly draftees, not volunteers. If you've never been drafted, have some empathy and listen to hear *how* what they say makes sense *to them*. Once you can get there, you then have a shot at changing those beliefs.

A metaphor that works well with those school-hating beliefs is to say (after you have empathetically heard their complaints) that school is like professional baseball: You play hard to work your way up through the lower (minor) leagues to one day drive a red convertible Corvette. A good effort in the lower leagues (middle school) gets you in shape for the next higher league (high school), which gets you in shape to make it in the major leagues (college/trade school/military). That last league can get you the keys to that convertible (some life goal) if you work hard. Kids can accept the "irrelevance" of school once they see it as a game to get you into the next game and then to a life you want. That can reduce the hating part. And if Corvettes are not their thing, try depicting education as something they are bound to want— freedom, aka autonomy: "You know, carpenters, chefs, and nurses can go about anywhere in the world they want and get a good job. Education can be airline tickets."

The red Corvette worked great for me.

Won't Do Schoolwork

"Schoolwork is irrelevant to my lifestyle."
—Author's son, age 13

Do:

✔ Stay calm. Know that there are countless other parents who wish their worst teen challenge was schoolwork.

✔ Know that Mother Nature has safety nets for kids who slack through high school, such as community college, technical school, or the military, any of which can suddenly look good to that growing {A} brain.

✔ View her avoidance as a *symptom*, not a *sin*.

✔ Know that most schoolwork avoiders are not happy campers, and most homework doers are. Somewhere inside of that skull, a doer—her {A} brain—is waiting to take control back from her {C}.

✔ Try to figure out what keeps that doer away from her desk (fear, depression, learning/organization problem, poor workspace, anger, and so on).

✔ Offer to help or, better yet, to get her help. Have you noticed how we shrinks are so amazingly more effective with *other* people's kids than our own? That parental disability applies to you as well.

✔ Suggest that she try not doing homework at home. (The library may work much better.)

✔ "Chunk" homework into 20 to 30 minute efforts with short movement breaks.

✔ Offer consequence-linked incentives such as earning (or failing to earn) computer time, money, and so on.

✔ Offer (don't force) nightly schoolwork assistance from you or a tutor. Accept your kid's ABY ("Anybody But You") helper mantra. That's smart.

✔ Set up a quiet, uncluttered, and well-lit homework space without electronics nearby. Bribe for that if you must.

✔ Ask for only a four-week trial to see how doing assignments works/feels.

✗ Offer incentives based on her *efforts*, not her grades.

Don't:

✗ Yell, nag, or threaten. As you've seen, those tricks never work.

✗ Fight bitterly ("You're such a loser!") over schoolwork. You can win a battle for her grades and lose the war for her heart.

✗ Ever quit. Your continued calm, loving concern will take root one day: "I'm still worried about how hard school seems for you. Let me know when you're ready to look at that."

✗ Do schoolwork for her. To her that can feel great in the moment and be crippling over time.

Job one is to get your emotions in hand before you deal with theirs. Your anger will only provide an easy diversion to fight over, enabling your kid to avoid taking a hard look at himself. Try seeing academic skills as tennis skills: They both take lots of practice, coaching, and effort, but neither can really be angrily forced—he has to want to do this. So go back to square one with him to find his {A} belief about why he should do well academically: "What's the point of your going to school? What's the payoff for *you*?" Once you establish his rationale for doing school ("To not be a bum" is fine for now), join forces with him to get to *his* goal, not yours. Without his involvement and commitment, your loving efforts might feel like anger and control and only make things worse.

His possible reasons for doing poorly are many and often complex, so get the experts involved if his poor academic achievement becomes a long-term problem. Assemble the school personnel (teachers, counselors, school psychologists, and so on) together in joint meetings where everyone, including your child, brainstorms to find solutions. (Bring snacks. The staff really appreciates that.) If all of your best efforts seem to hit brick walls, don't despair and go nuts or quit, but don't go away either. Remember that your parenting mission is not to control your teen but to teach him to control himself, and that is a long-term effort. In that light, as parents of teenagers, we are in the failure business. We are here to help our kids learn powerful lessons from their failures to help them to eventually succeed with themselves: "Hey, Mom—I just discovered something. I actually can't study with my TV, computer, phone, and iPod all running. Do you think that scientists have discovered this yet?" Beyond all else, do not let worries about grades become family wars where you lose your connections with your kid.

His grades are important, but they are a *secondary* concern. Your priority is keeping close to his heart (his values and beliefs) through the As *and* the Fs. He can always make up for bad grades later in life. Lost love is gone forever. Your anger can trigger power and control struggles and only give him additional reasons to *not* do his schoolwork, and his subsequent feelings of rejection can lead you to be reading other sections of this part of the book about crises far worse than schoolwork.

All kids want to achieve, so view his reluctance as a sign of another problem you must ferret out and then try to remedy. For example, what parents often label as "lazy" is just a cover for kids who think it's less painful to flunk themselves (by not trying) than to get flunked after having tried. Their {C} brain is running things. But just like that baseball player who's too scared to get up to bat, your kid will never see if he can get a hit until he takes some swings. And you never know what kind of coaching he needs until someone analyzes his swing. So your immediate goal is to get your kid into that batter's box, not to get a hit but just to take a few swings.

First, stop doing all you've likely been doing (yelling, threatening, nagging) and apologize for having made him feel worse. Get yourself calm by knowing that lots of kids who duck their potential in high school find it waiting for them in tech schools, community colleges, and the military. For now, do that trick where you hook the {A} part of him: "I hear you when you say that you hate schoolwork and will never, ever do it. I know that's what most of you feels. But is there a small part of you, perhaps just a 5 percent part, that thinks maybe you should do schoolwork? Yes? Cool! Can I talk to that part for a minute?" Ask that {A} part why *he* thinks he should do his schoolwork, and keep asking until you get answers reflecting *his own* belief system, not yours: "How do *you* think that schoolwork might help *your* life?" Once he admits that he wants to do well for himself, propose some of the steps noted previously to help him to get at his real avoidance issue.

Ask his {A} brain to push hard for only a short time, perhaps four weeks, just to see how he feels after trying. This helps his task looks less daunting than a total life commitment, and often after just two weeks of trying, his good feelings (intrinsic pay-offs) from doing his job will keep him keeping on. If you offer incentives, be sure that they reward his *effort* (time and energy) and not his outcome (grades). The grades will follow effort, and the real gold is that effort. Finally, set up a meeting for you, him, and his teachers to jointly discuss what needs to be done (tutoring, educational testing, doing homework at school, and so on).

If his schoolwork performance stays spotty, see a helper (an LMHP). In addition, don't yell or nag, but don't quit on him either. Softly revisit this from time to time since time is on your side as his {A} brain wires in. Tell him that you are always there to help him if/when he decides it's time to get out of the dugout and take a shot in that batter's box. Softly remind him that no one in the history of the game ever got a hit without stepping into the box.

Don't hesitate to offer those incentives for good efforts. While incentives sound like a mercenary contamination of something that many hold sacred (education), this trick can kick-start your resistant learner to take a shot at overcoming his initial fear. As he experiences success, that "joy of learning" and achievement stuff can begin to grow within him. In the interim, you must accept that bumper sticker premise that he and he alone will ultimately decide if any changes will occur. That's just the fact. We must accept our teenagers for who they are in relation to school, and then tweak that as best we can while we wait for the intellectual awakening and study discipline that almost always eventually blossom—if we're wise enough to not go toe-to-toe in bitter, judgmental, and demoralizing rages with them. Our anger only delays or kills off that wondrous maturation, and it can bring on terrible new problems of behavior that can make the old issues of achievement look like stupid things over which to have started a war.

Mother Nature provides safety nets for school-challenged adolescents. It's called maturity. I once received a letter from Michele, a brilliant high school underachiever with whom I had worked. It read: "Hey Doc Mike! Guess where I'm graduating from next week. No, it's not [the local juvenile prison]. It's NYU! Ha! You'd never have guessed that I could do that, right? Tell the truth . . ." Michele went on to describe how she had gone to a community college, learned the discipline of study, and then parlayed that into a degree from a great university.

I was never able to "cure" Michele. But I was able to help her parents to shift their approach from the anger and rejection of punishment to the support and acceptance of love. It was very hard for them, for they believed as most of us do that it is an act of love to rage at a school-challenged child. It is not. They never saw Michele on an honor roll in high school, but they also never saw her on an inmate roll in rehab or jail. And then they watched her graduate from NYU on the only timetable that really works— our kids', not our own.

After telling you the wonderful tale of how Michele's story ended at NYU, I need to possibly rain on a parade of yours that might be killing your kid's school motivation. Remember way back at the beginning of the book when I made a snarky comment about my perhaps not guaranteeing your kid's admission to Princeton University even if I could? That's because *not everyone should go to college.* College for everyone is a strange idea that evolved over the past five decades to become a universal goal. If it was working well, I wouldn't be opposed, but it's not. As of this writing, more than *half* of our kids who start college *never complete it.* Those that do often find that their degree gets them offered the day shift at the convenience store. Those that quit or fail often dejectedly shuffle off those campuses feeling like losers, and they are carrying letters in their backpacks delineating the tens of thousands of dollars they spent and/or owe for a process that made them feel terrible.

This "college as 13th grade" nonsense needs to be challenged. If your goal for your kid is life happiness, focus on what that means *to your kid*. That might include college. Or a trade school, or technical school, or the military—whatever fits their identity. I've known physicians who absolutely love their work, and I've known some who absolutely hate their work. It's the same with cops, soldiers, chefs, electricians, and about every other job you can think of. Many kids get demoralized thinking that college is the only path to success and happiness, because that's what we pound into them starting in preschool, yet some wise part of them senses that college is not for them. Thus, a lot of school resistance can be reduced when we broaden their options to include "not college."

Be sure to chat about kids in Europe who usually take a "gap year" before heading to university (a practice that is becoming more accepted in America). Research that concept. That's a year when kids do important things around the world while they grow, think, and mature in ways that help them figure out who the heck they really are and what they might want to do in the world. If that is college, they are not a year behind; they are *years ahead* since when they do enroll these kids tend to be much better students who do much less partying and are much more serious about schoolwork. That's because now they are directing their own path, regardless of where it may lead. Seeing that intrinsic, resilience-building motivation tells us parents that it's time to retire, since our job is about done.

NINE

Sex and Dating Issues

"So, Mom, Dad was the first guy you had sex with, right?
Mom? Mom? Did you hear me? I asked if . . ."
—Many parents' most feared question

I f you are reading this, you might have just discovered that your
child is now a sexual creature. Welcome to your nightmare.
You see, I understand. You always knew that your girl or boy
would be a woman or man one day, but really, you didn't. You
always harbored this secret, bizarre belief that your child would
not be as sexually driven as you were as a teen, that somehow
your kid would rise above all that stuff until at least age, I don't
know, 25 or 30. And you were comforted by knowing that, with
a little luck, you might be dead by then anyway. So no worries.
Am I right?

Your level of denial might not be as radical as my own, but
most parents deny their kids' sexuality to some extent, which is
exactly what we should not do. For the truly frightening reality
is that as sexually preoccupied as we were as adolescents, our
teens are worse. Not because they're worse people, but because
they're in a worse culture, one that seems obsessed with all things

sex. They have been pounded with sexual training from the day they first gaped at a TV set from their playpen, being powerfully programmed to believe that the primary aspect of their worth and function on this planet is sexual.

Sex education at school is helpful, but it's not the complete answer. Sure, they get the form and function stuff there, but that's not nearly enough. What the schools cannot (and should not) provide are the truly "sexy"(important) parts of sex—namely, the aspects of values, codes, and moral identity. Those must remain the purview of the parent. "OK, Dr. Bradley," you sigh. "*You* try having the sex talk with my kid. He puts his hands over his ears and sings the national anthem until I stop." Of course he does. You see, "the sex talk" should actually be 10,000 mini-talks, small and casual exchanges that begin at birth and continue forever, not one five-hour marathon in the kitchen. The topic should become normalized and frequently referenced for years in small snippets of 30-second chats. These could be prompted by screen images: "This movie shows that prostitute as cool and having a good time. Do you think that's the way it really is for those women?" Or by song lyrics: "This song says it's cool to be a pimp. What do you think about that?" Or by news articles: "That magazine says that rape is a sex crime. Do you think rape is about sex or about violence?"

Much of the talk should actually be wordless, as we allow our kids to see our own sexual values in action. What exactly do we display to our children? Do we treat people with sexual dignity, or do we leer and make provocative jokes? Do we respect our partners, or do we like to flirt? Are we faithful? Do we dress appropriately, or do we try to draw sexual attention? Think hard about these things because in the minds of our children, our actions will out-shout our words every time.

If you've been doing none of this right (as is true for too many of us), is it too late? Not at all. In fact, it's even more effective to start this approach while you're dealing with one of the scenarios below, since now the topic is so very real to your child. Remember, sex and dating are rarely fatal diseases and most often become dangerous only when they're ignored. You managed to survive as a teen, and so will your kid. It just doesn't feel that way when you're the parent.

Dating a Jerk

"Johnny loves me sooo much that he gets crazy jealous if I see my friends. So I cut them off."

—Alise, age 13

Do:

✔ Know that now is the time for cool diplomacy, not angry mandates.

✔ Know that forbidden love is always the "best" love (to a teen).

✔ Know that you're likely seeing only a small part of the craziness.

✔ Know that boys *and* girls can be controlling and abusive.

✔ Know that if you don't skillfully handle these relationships, they can become *lifelong* killers of resilience and creators of stress.

✔ Watch for signs of physical abuse with girls *and* boys (bruises, welts, injury-concealing clothing/makeup, wearing huge sunglasses all the time).

✔ Watch for signs of emotional abuse with girls *and* boys (withdrawal from friends, activities, family time; poor hygiene; changes in appetite/sleep).

✔ Calmly raise your concerns to your child.

✔ Impose safety limits without telling your teen whom to love.

✔ Invite the jerk into your house at every opportunity. (Keep your friends close and your enemies closer.)

✔ Allow your kid to safely learn about bad relationships (a thing better learned at age 16 than 36).

✔ Forbid contact if she admits to being physically abused, and call the police.

✔ Immediately get your child to an LMHP if you see evidence of abuse or crippling control that she denies.

Don't:

✘ Outright forbid the relationship (unless there are physical risks).

✘ Underestimate the power of teen love or the deficits of teen brains (see Chapter 3).

✘ Do nothing (or your kid will assume that this crazy behavior is OK).

✘ Criticize or demean the jerk to your child (unless you want a new in-law).

Incredibly, at least one-fourth of our daughters (and many of our sons) find themselves trapped in an abusive/controlling relationship before they escape high school. The antidote to that epidemic seems counterintuitive to us parents. For example, do you know how to magically transform a dislikable, abusive creep into the most desirable partner on the face of the planet? Forbid your teen from seeing the jerk. That's a surefire way to take what might have been a bizarre but passing fancy and turn it into a Romeo and Juliet love story that will fire up her {C} brain into a blast furnace. Do what you must to keep your kid safe from her {C} brain ("But he loves me"), and remember that teaching is your first priority. But if you just forbid all contact, the learning always ends and the running sometimes begins (as in fleeing to Mexico and getting pregnant in the bargain). That learning is critical to helping your kid to avoid the next controlling jerk, when the stakes might include a 10-year marriage and two small babies.

Impose safety restrictions as you must, but don't stop the relationship (unless there is physical abuse) or disrespect the jerk to your child: "Honey, I worry that things are not so good in your relationship. Whom you date is your business, but your safety is mine, so I'll ask you to only see him here or when you're with a group of friends. He's welcome in our home anytime you like. In fact, how about asking him for dinner on Sunday?" Set up a "compare and contrast" exercise for your teen by getting Mr./Ms. Wrong to sulkily sit at your Sunday dinner table in the unforgiving light of day next to positive, happy, well-adjusted role models (like an older sib). The jerk's nasty behaviors will stick out like a sore thumb for your child to ponder. Then sit back and wait *without commenting*.

I happen to know (professionally and personally) only too well that this is easier said than done, but I also know that time works to your advantage. The jerks start to lose the super-attracting quality of being hated by parents, and their imperfections become impossible for your kid's {A} brain to overlook. Offer an ear when you see a tear, but don't press hard for information. Let them share what they wish. And if your child tells you a story that makes you want to punch the jerk, just listen quietly and ask what your teen thinks and feels. Punching (or even insulting) the jerk will stop the learning. Let your kid work this out so that this crucial resilience lesson lasts a lifetime.

Having Sex

Do:

✔ Stay cool. Your calm composure and wise words can be life-saving.

✔ Know that the pressures on kids to be sexual have never been higher.

✔ Know that the mythology of "casual/harmless" sex is rampant among supposedly smart teens.

✔ Know that rates of sexually transmitted diseases (STDs) are high among adolescents.

✔ Know that girls are often the sexual aggressors in middle school and yet have mixed feelings or regrets about having sex.

✔ Call for a "team meeting" that includes the parents of your kid's boyfriend/girlfriend. (Share these pages of the book with them.)

✔ Ask what the couple's plans are for a possible pregnancy (this is a very real possibility), and have them think about how that would change their lives.

✔ Be sure they are using birth control. Tell them the safety and effectiveness rates for teen birth control (about 90 percent) and the failure rates for teen-parent families (almost 100 percent).

✔ Eliminate rendezvous opportunities if she seems determined to continue having sex, but only as a last resort.

✔ See an LMHP if you hit a wall.

Don't:

✗ Go crazy. Your screaming and yelling can be life-destroying.

✗ Think that teens are old enough for this. (They just look that way.)

✗ Play the morality/values cards first. (Those talks can come later.)

✗ Totally forbid her relationship or she might head for South America with him. (See the previous section on "Dating a Jerk.")

✗ Cave in and allow her to continue having sex. Lives are literally at stake. Some haven't yet arrived.

Your first step is to study those Don'ts. Teens in love/lust are not able to respond well to lectures about religion or morality—at least not quickly enough for this crisis—so teach, don't preach. Screaming at her to not have sex can make that very act even more attractive as a way to pay you back. Even just forbidding her relationship can fan the small flames of desire into a firestorm of pregnancy risk and encourage her to run away on a romantic "Romeo and Juliet misunderstood teens" adventure. But cold statistics on STDs and pregnancy can chill passion pretty effectively. This is especially so for girls who are anti-abortion (who get to raise the kid for the rest of their lives) and boys who feel the same (and get to pay for the kid for the rest of their lives). Abortion or adoption can be very traumatic as well, facts that they've likely witnessed with their peers.

These horny teens have heard all about the risks of having sex, but all of that information they got in school has been neatly packed away in a distant region of their brains for the duration of the romance. So you've got to objectively rain on their passion parade with the risk data they've already heard, but which will sound very different now that they're staring down the possible barrel of a positive pregnancy or STD test. We learn best when it gets real. How did you figure this stuff out? Right. Me too.

Restrict her freedom as you must for safety, but do this only as a last resort since it will only control her behavior for a few weeks and might push her further down the path of unprotected sex and running away. Instead, try shaping her {A} beliefs for a lifetime. Unfortunately for parents, teaching kids works best with calm conversation exactly at the time when you want to yell the most. Yell at your kickboxing partner while you're crazy, and talk with your kid when you're calm.

If you can negotiate that magic balance of safety and auton-omy, time will provide your eventual antidote since most teen romances have the shelf life of unrefrigerated whole milk. To help tolerate your pain, know that these crazy relationships are how we all learn the skills we need to one day make a great life-partner choice. There simply is no easy path. So think about keeping friends close and enemies closer: "He's welcome here anytime, and you can hang out in groups with him, but going to his house is out of the question for now. We'll visit this again when you're older."

As scary as this nightmare is for you, understand that her sexual activity (without pregnancy) is very much a gift (though a hated one) if you can view this behavior as a symptom, not a sin. Now you have a shot at the most powerful type of teaching that teens can experience, namely teaching while the lesson is relevant to their lives. Your lesson plan must be to shape her {A} belief system about the relative gain/risk of sexual activity so that next time she might think twice—not just with this "once-in-a-lifetime forever-love soul mate" but with the 10 others she's going to meet in the next 10 years as she defines her true sexual identity and values. Your moral judgments on her character will kill the learning. Your unconditional love will make it powerful.

TEN

Social Issues

sn't it amazing? There you were thinking that your teenager
was doing most of her learning on weekdays from 8 AM to
3 PM, and suddenly it hit you that she is enrolled in *two* schools,
not one. There's the important one you already knew about, the
one with the smelly gym, scary bathrooms, and bad food. And
then there's the *really* important one that you just began to no-
tice: her "social school." That caught you by surprise, didn't it?
That's because we parents tend to toss our adolescent's relationship issues into that same low-priority basket that holds her
choices of toothpaste, music, and movies. After all, how important can peers be to a kid? Answer: *exponentially more important
to her than yours are to you.* And they represent a critical brick
in the wall of building her lifelong resilience.

Much like an ocean reef, a teenager's social network provides
a vast diversity of interaction, an incredibly rich source of learning and growth. This "social school" is a living learning

laboratory where she gets to observe and test concepts that are much more important than anything she'll ever see in chemistry class. In "social school," she learns about loyalty, respect, values, trust, character, compassion, negotiation, selflessness, codes of behavior, love, and a few other similar trivial things that all build resilience.

This is another of those examples of how your kid is in a very different place than you, and your not appreciating that can hurt her. When it comes to social issues, your schooling is mostly over. You largely know who you are, what you believe, and what things hold value for you. Because you know these things, you have lots of supports that help you to not be excessively affected (have more resilience) in the face of negative social events such as arguing with a friend, being excluded from a group, or being hassled by a jerk. If things go bad at the golf course, you've still got your life partner, work friends, neighbors, self-confidence, and so on. But your kid has few of those anchors and thus gets tossed around a lot harder by her social storms. The irony is that instead of avoiding those squalls, she needs to sail head-on through them to learn to eventually be more secure. Isn't that how you learned?

Sharp teeth and dangerous coral are also hidden in that reef, and they can puncture a teen's fragile self-worth in a New York minute and even put her at risk of physical harm. The best and the worst of her world will be the social part. So how do we parents protect our novice sailors and yet allow them to learn?

The fact is that the more we big fish (parents) interfere with life on the reef, the less the little fish learn. So if you decide to intervene in your kid's relationships, do so knowing that all learning will likely end, and she may need to complete the lesson later on in life. When it comes to social issues, "Let It Be" should be our parental theme song, although that's admittedly a tune that sounds great until we start to see sharp teeth coming toward our kid. "Uh-oh" moments like those are when we earn those big bucks that parents get paid to decide if and when and how to intervene. The sections below will help you to do just that.

What are the general guidelines? Mostly to do less, not more. Provide an empathetic ear, not an expert mouth. Remember that trial and error is usually the most effective kind of learning as long as the learner survives to use the knowledge. Ask soft questions and offer quiet observations instead of taking hard control of your kid's social life: "Honey, I worry that things are not too cool at Susan's house. What do you think?"

Finally, when you are about to belly flop into that reef not so much to protect your kid but really to help *you* feel better, consider my wife's words of wisdom that she uses to remind me that we want our kids to learn these tough lessons while they are still in our home. She sings "Let It Be," adding a line: "*Better at 14 than at 40.*"

Being Bullied

Do:

✔ Know that bullying, like drug use, can cause changes in behavior (social withdrawal, school avoidance, sleep/food issues, moodiness). The cause is often hidden since bullying causes shame.

✔ Know that bullying can be physical, verbal, cyber, and silent (shunning).

✔ Know that verbal/cyber/silent bullying can hurt more than physical hitting.

✔ Know that what adult victims call "harassment" and "assault," kid victims are told is "teasing," "normal," "inevitable," and "toughening."

✔ Know that bullying wounds are linked with depression, shyness, truancy, and suicide.

✔ Know that, contrary to the myth, bullies are usually popular with their peers and with themselves (i.e., have good self-esteem).

✔ Know that bullies are usually bigger, more well-liked, and stronger than their victims (so it's a movie myth to solve the problem with fistfights).

✔ Know that your teenager might be too ashamed to tell you what's been happening.

✔ Know that bullying is best stopped by long-term, repeated, schoolwide programs, not by individual bully/victim confrontations or mediations.

✔ Know that each victim must find his own way to cope and respond.

✔ Offer your supportive, connecting ear, not your emotionally distancing advice.

✔ Offer to call the school, and insist on this if the bullying is extreme, but . . .

✔ . . . Know that the school might make things worse if the staff is not well trained in bullying intervention.

✔ Know that bullying peaks in middle school and then slowly ebbs with each passing year.

✔ Ask if he ever thinks about hurting himself or about plans for violent revenge. If he says yes, secure any weapons and see an LMHP immediately to evaluate those potentials.

✔ Consider bribing to get him off social media for a few months if he's being cyberbullied (which is where most of this savagery occurs).

Don't:

✗ Think that fighting is the answer for your kid, *especially* if it was for you.

✗ Think that you know what her answer should be.

✗ Minimize this torture as "normal."

✗ Let your own anger or disappointment in her (because she won't fight?) keep her from sharing her own self-anger and disappointment.

✗ Call the school without her permission, at least initially. (Schools sometimes make things worse, and she needs to have as much control right now as possible.)

✗ Forget that she needs your love and support, not your hand-to-hand training.

Here's some breaking news: America's pastime for today's teens is bullying, not baseball. More than half of our kids are being targeted at one time or another, and many are too ashamed to admit it. It's so common that we adults (who'd file charges if we were treated the same as our teens) don't really see it anymore. In fact, we often romanticize bullying as a normal and strengthening process, one that "builds resilience" like boot camp. It does not. These victims are children, not soldiers, and they're draftees, not volunteers. They're trapped in their schools and neighborhoods with jerks for whom we adults would get restraining orders. Think of yourself in prison and you'll get the idea. Bullying is a poison that kills resilience and promotes dangerous levels of stress.

So you agree that the damage to your kid from bullying is so great that you must do something. But what? You must realize that retaliation (fistfighting, insulting back) very rarely works and usually makes things worse. Win or lose that one battle and the viciousness of the war usually just increases. And if you intend to get the school to do something, you'd better first see what that something might be. If the staff talks about schoolwide training programs, push for those (they are very effective). If they talk only about punishing the bully and/or forced mediation ("OK, now shake hands and let's be friends"), let your kid decide. The outcomes of these options are often worse than doing nothing.

Bullying is more a complex social/community/group process than a fight between two competitors, so the only real solution is changing how bullying is seen in that community. Without that change in community/bystander attitude ("Yo, dude! That's not funny, man"), there is probably not much good that the school can do for your suffering child. Moreover, electronics (as discussed in Chapter 2) have indeed provided nuclear weapons to the bullying terrorists. Several instances of attempted and completed suicide in America have been attributed to cyberbullying.

But there is a lot that you can do on your own, with a system I call "Outlast the Bastards." First, give your kid your caring ear, that most healing and least used of all parent tools. Listening well is perhaps 50 percent of the cure. Agree with him that this is incredibly painful. Next (after he's poured out his pain), point out to him that this insanity peaks in middle school, decreases through high school, and virtually disappears in college. Telling your kid that in college bullies are the ones who get laughed at and shunned gives him hope that life gets better (which it most definitely does). Then ask if he'd like your help in developing some strategies to survive until then. Do some brainstorming to make a list of all the options from which he can pick and choose.

Start by suggesting use of small thermonuclear devices and work downward from there (humor helps a lot). Have him evaluate strategies such as firmly saying "Please stop that!" (this works more often than most think), ignoring (this is easier said than done), avoiding, soft retorting (e.g., shrugs and saying "whatever"), traveling with friends, and making new friends through activities. That lengthy list—even if some of the strategies aren't practical—will help him to feel a bit of control just when he desperately needs some.

Try to keep your mission in mind. Remember that your priority is *not* to solve his problem but to get his {A} brain learning the skills to take care of his {C} brain emotions for the 10,000 challenges you will not be around to fix. This develops a core piece of resilience and the skill to control his stress levels for the rest of his life. *It doesn't matter if his first response choice doesn't work.* It matters that he keeps reevaluating and trying new options until he finds *his* best one, not yours.

Ask your child to get quiet and hear what her {P} brain is saying to her about her. The odds are high that her {P} has taken up where the jerks left off, calling her loser, ugly, fat, skinny, friendless. Point out that this is like having a bully in our heads 24/7, one that she needs to stand up to. Ask her {A} to respond to the taunts of her {P}: "I hear part of you saying you have zero friends. Is that true?" "I hear that {P} saying you are ugly. Is that true?" When/if she says "I am ugly," answer that you hear her 4-year-old brain (her {C}) saying that she *feels* ugly. Ask if her 14-year-old brain (her {A}) *thinks* that she is ugly. Help her to distinguish those voices and ask her which set of beliefs is better for decisions: what we *feel* or what we *think*.

If she's too reactive to the taunting, use therapist Fred Hanna's "Freedom Challenge."[1] Point out that when you react to bullies, they own you. Reframe the act of maintaining her composure and coolly walking away not as cowardice but as a victory for freedom since the jerk no longer controls her reactions. That's a very tough thing to do, but it might be her least painful option.

Repeat this drill periodically to adapt to the changes in your kid's growing maturity and in the nature of the bullying. Most of all, keep a sharp eye and a caring ear out for the devastating depression that can result from this torture. Then hunker down with your kid to "Outlast the Bastards." Speaking as a veteran "bastard outlaster," I can personally attest that living well is indeed the best revenge.

Is Painfully Shy

Do:

✔ Know that if shyness is interfering with your kid living her life as she wants, her shyness is a *disorder*, not a characteristic.

✔ Know that shyness is not who she *is* (her {A} brain) but how she *feels* (her {C} brain).

✔ Know that painfully shy kids usually feel bad about themselves.

✔ Know that shyness can be a biochemical disorder and/or a learned response (from being bullied or abused), and it can seriously damage her social/emotional development and resilience.

✔ Know that 50 percent of adults report having struggled with shyness.

✔ Ask her if she's OK with being so shy, but go softly (she might feel too ashamed to talk about it).

✔ Try to help her see shyness as a limiting characteristic, not as her limited character.

✔ Keep affirming the real positives about her (not empty platitudes).

✔ Ask her if she'd like to do something to change.

✔ Offer incentives to be more social (hanging out, group activities with peers).

✔ Contact her school to see if they have "friendship clubs" that help shy kids.

✔ Tell her that many famous folks found great lives by doing things to shake off their shyness (see www.shakeyourshyness.com). Note that most of these people report *working* at it by using their {A} brain to overcome {C} fears.

✔ Model and share your own anti-shyness techniques (greeting others warmly, asking others about themselves). Tell her about how you force yourself to attend social events you want to duck and then are glad that you went.

Don't.

. . . .

✘ Believe that he prefers living like this.

✘ Joke or mock him about his shyness, or allow others to.

✘ Nag, demand, or try to force him to change.

✘ Just ignore it and hope that it goes away.

Excessive shyness is less a part of personality and more a limiter of personality. It is not who a teen is but rather a serious condition that prevents your kid from being who she is and from becoming who she wants to be. Left untreated, it may just go away on its own, but its costs can be substantial in the interim. Shyness can rob her of so much of her teen life that it can prevent her from achieving the number one job of adolescence: figuring out who she is.

Research the Web with your kid for the amazing stories of successful people who struggled (and who continue to struggle) with painful shyness. A very short list includes historical figures such as Albert Einstein, Theodore Roosevelt, Eleanor Roosevelt, Thomas Jefferson, and Ulysses S. Grant; entertainers such as Brad Pitt, Julia Roberts, David Bowie, Michelle Pfeiffer, David Letterman, George Harrison, Gloria Estefan, Jim Carrey, Tom Hanks, and Kevin Costner; and athletes such as Mia Hamm and Cathy Rigby. And those are just the ones secure enough to admit to their shyness. Then ask your child to let you know when she's ready to attack this problem with the aid of a helper (an LMHP).

In the interim, use every opportunity to openly model and share with her your own four-step process of confronting shyness. First, label the irrational, anticipatory fear of your {C} brain: "A silly part of me, my {C} brain, says that all of the other people at this party will hate me." Second, check in with your {A} brain: "The smarter part of me, my {A}, predicts that I'll probably have fun and be glad I went. That's what always happens." Third, make the decision: "I guess I have to decide which of my brains is smarter." And finally, do the post-event evaluation (learning): either "I'm really mad at myself for listening to my {C} brain and not going. I heard it was fun," or hopefully, "I'm so glad that I trusted my {A} brain and went. I had a great time."

Until your kid signals that she's ready, focus extra time and attention on helping her to remember all that's truly good about her, such as her accomplishments and/or her good character traits (empathy, compassion, and so on). Be sure these are real things, not pie-in-the-sky platitudes such as "You're the most wonderful girl in the whole wide world." Work with her to find activities where she can socialize in a less stressful way (e.g., tutoring younger kids, community service). Start with the least intimidating ones and work upward. Competitive sports might initially be a bridge too far. Volunteering at the food bank might be more doable.

Be sure to share with her the life story and powerful words uttered by a painfully shy person who ended up accomplishing a thing or two in her life: "No one can make you feel inferior without your consent." That was Eleanor Roosevelt.

Epilogue

Congratulations! Your training has ended and your adventure now begins. Parenting adolescents in this new age is indeed an adventure in every sense of that word, especially the one about it being a transformative experience where we end as someone who had not yet existed when we began. My personal goal of getting you in shape for that challenge had me beating you over the head about your parental mission, strategies, and tactics, all designed to build the magic of resilience in your teenager. But that left little room to dwell with awe on the big picture here, one that justifies all of that hard discipline I ask of you: *This is about parenting a child into adulthood, about teaching another human being who will end this adventure as someone who had not yet existed when it began, someone who will be more influenced by you than anything else in the cosmos.*

That big picture should take our breath away daily, but it likely has not for a long time. If it ever did, it was when we reverently first held our new child in our arms, joyfully overwhelmed by the incredible miracle of the circle of life. Then we got so swept away by the grinding frustration of day-to-day parenting that we lost the essence of our task as defined by its *sacredness*. Parenting must never be about creating an Ivy League freshman. It must be about creating the *parent of your grandchildren*. This must first be about their *hearts*, not their resumes.

This is as close as we get to touching the face of infinity. What each of us does tonight as a parent will become part of the legacy we pass down forever. What do you want to leave behind? Anger, disappointment, judgment, pain, sadness? That's what we bequeath forever when we focus only upon what our teens are not. Would you instead prefer to hand down treasures such as acceptance, patience, humor, joy, and tolerance, *especially* in the face of provocation? Those heirlooms are created by cherishing our children *as they are* versus *whom we want them to be*. That act is a thing called love, which ultimately is the most powerful tactic of all.

Heroes offer up their lives not from hatred of an enemy but for love of their sisters and brothers. Gallantry can't happen in calm, peaceful settings. For heroic parents and soldiers, true valor occurs amid fear, pain, chaos, and soul-crushing exhaustion. So try not to fear the bad times quite so much. Ironically, they will give you the chance to be so much more than you could have ever imagined or would have ever attempted to be on your own. During those dark days, that kid who seems so hell-bent on making you insane is *even now* watching how you handle yourself. She is learning how to be when *her* daughter makes *her* insane.

To help you with your heroic efforts, I leave you with my four best parenting tricks. The first is an attitude that comes courtesy of the late Yogi Berra. Yogi had some very dark baseball days in 1973 when he was managing the New York Mets and the team was in last place. He said something offhandedly that has become a mantra for struggling folks everywhere: *It ain't over till it's over.* Later that season, and against all odds, the team won its division and made it to the World Series. Personally and professionally, I've seen the wisdom of Yogi's attitude countless times when kids who seemed so hopeless made amazing comebacks as young adults. Almost always, they had parents who in their own dark days would shrug just like Yogi and say, "It ain't over till it's over." And then they'd press on.

The second parenting trick is to quote Colin Powell, a homework-refusing, underachieving, high school C student who became a four-star general and Secretary of State. In the military, I heard his leadership mantra only about 10 times a day—*"Perpetual optimism is a force multiplier"*—meaning that a smaller force of soldiers with high morale can overwhelm a much larger, dispirited force. That's more true in parenting than in soldiering. You must always look toward the optimistic parenting possibility *especially* when times are tough because that's when we often feel hopelessly outnumbered and outgunned.

To help you to do that, I share my third trick, one I cheerfully named the "Deathbed Exercise." Coming home every night during our family's tough teen times, I would pause for a moment in the garage before opening the inner door. You see, being Irish, ex-military, and the survivor of 16 years of Catholic education has left me with an amazing tendency to and capability of going nuts to exert control over chaotic situations. That includes things such as my son's bedroom ("My bed's still there, Dad. See? It's under the pizza boxes, I think") or meeting my daughter's latest Mr. Wonderful ("Genghis is in middle management—at the tattoo parlor"). No longer carrying a sidearm, I'd instead pause, take a breath, and ask myself the smartest question I will ever ask myself: *"Yo, Mike. When you are on your deathbed reviewing your life, how will you feel then about what you are about to do tonight?"* That sobers me up real quick. I'd point to whomever/whatever is in the sky, say, "Thanks! Got it!" and open the door. I'd go find my son, give him a hard hug, tell him I love him, ask how his world is going, and listen without criticizing. Then, I might ask, as I'd asked 10,000 times before, "Ross, is it possible to take the food packages out of your room before they crawl out on their own?" He'd laugh and say, "Sure, Dad." We repeated that drill until the day he finally moved out. That's one small example showing how resilience parenting is mostly about smart priorities (e.g., heart first, orderliness second), methodologies (e.g., be what you want to see, be careful what you go to war over), and patience (e.g., have faith that the seeds you plant with love will one day sprout with joy).

"But Dr. B," you quickly point out, "that didn't work. Your son was a total slob while he was with you. He never learned how to be neat." My answer is in the report of my stunned daughter following her first visit to my son's new home: "Dad, you're not gonna believe this. Ross is like the *neat freak* in that house! He's always cleaning up after his roommates and lecturing them about keeping things neat!" As I listened to my daughter, it would be only a slight exaggeration to say I was ready to go if that was my time to die.

My fourth and best personal parenting trick is humor, the darker, sanity-preserving kind practiced by soldiers in foxholes, cops in squad cars, and exhausted parents of teenagers trying to maintain the self-discipline of resilience parenting just when they most want to go berserk. Cindy and I have a favorite cartoon we've referenced late at night only about a thousand times, drawn by Peter C. Vey. He's done lots of work for publications like *The New Yorker* and *Mad Magazine*—a perfect resume for a parenting commentator, no? I was clued into this gem at a seminar I was doing by a retired pediatrician/parent, a man with the "eyes of age" that have seen and experienced about everything about parenting. He said it kept him and his wife sane through their kids' tough teen years. I suggest you get it as a poster (it's available online) and hang it in your kitchen. The scene is a middle-age couple reading serenely in their living room with the wife raising her head and saying, "Now that the kids are in jail, maybe we can take that vacation we always wanted."

Good luck out there, keep your head down, and keep laughing!

—*Doc Mike*

APPENDIX

WANT TO LEARN MORE?

Aiken, Mary. *The Cyber Effect: A Pioneering Cyber-psychologist Explains How Human Behavior Changes Online*. Spiegel & Grau, 2016.

Antony, Martin M. and Richard P. Swinson. *The Shyness & Social Anxiety Workbook: Proven, Step-by-Step Techniques for Overcoming Your Fear*. New Harbinger Publications, 2008.

Basso, Michael J. *The Underground Guide to Teenage Sexuality*. Fairview Press, 2003

Bast, Donna S. *Teens and Computers . . . What's a Parent to Do? A Basic Guide to Social Networking, Instant Messaging, Chat, Email, Computer Set-up, and More*. CreateSpace, 2007.

Blanco, Jodee. *Please Stop Laughing at Us: One Survivor's Extraordinary Quest to Prevent School Bullying*. BenBella Books, 2008.

Borba, Michele. *UnSelfie: Why Empathetic Kids Succeed in Our All-About-Me World*. Touchstone, 2016.

Bradley, Michael J. *Yes, Your Parents Are Crazy!: A Teen Survival Guide*. Harbor Press, 2004.

Bright, Neil. *Rethinking Everything: Personal Growth through Transactional Analysis*. Roman & Littlefield, 2015.

Christen, Carol and Richard N. Bolles. *What Color Is Your Parachute? For Teens, 2nd Edition: Discovering Yourself, Defining Your Future*. Ten Speed Press, 2011.

Coloroso, Barbara. *The Bully, the Bullied, and the Bystander: From Preschool to High School—How Parents and Teachers Can Help Break the Cycle of Violence*. William Morrow, 2009.

Crandell, Christy. *Lost & Found: A Mother and Son Find Victory Over Teen Drug Addiction*. Pascoe Publishing, 2006.

Ginsburg, Kenneth R. *Building Resilience in Children and Teens: Giving Kids Roots and Wings, Raising Kids to Thrive: Balancing Love with Expectations and Protection with Trust.* American Academy of Pediatrics, 2015.

Hipp, Earl. *Fighting Invisible Tigers: Stress Management for Teens.* Free Spirit Publishing, 2008.

James, Muriel and Dorothy Jonge-Ward. *Born to Win: Transactional Analysis With Gestalt Experiments, 25th Anniversary Edition.* Da Capo Press, 1996.

Jensen, Frances E. and Amy Ellis Nutt. *The Teenage Brain: A Neuroscientist's Survival Guide to Raising Adolescents and Young Adults.* Harper Paperbacks, 2016.

Kohn, Alfie. *The Homework Myth: Why Our Kids Get Too Much of a Bad Thing.* Da Capo Lifelong Books, 2006.

Luthar, Suniya S., ed. *Resilience and Vulnerability: Adaptation in the Context of Childhood Adversities.* Cambridge University Press, 2003.

Murray, Jill. *But I Love Him: Protecting Your Teen Daughter from Controlling, Abusive Dating Relationships.* Regan Books, 2001.

Schaefer, Dick. *Choices and Consequences: What to Do When a Teenager Uses Alcohol/Drugs.* Hazelden, 2010.

Seaward, Brian Luke and Linda K. Bartlett. *Hot Stones & Funny Bones: Teens Helping Teens Cope with Stress & Anger.* HCI Teens, 2002.

Siegel, Daniel J. *Brainstorm: The Power and Purpose of the Teenage Brain.* Tarcher Perigree, 2015.

Stepp, Laura Sessions. *Unhooked: How Young Women Pursue Sex, Delay Love* and *Lose at Both.* Riverhead Books, 2008.

Zimbardo, Philip G. *Shyness: What It Is, What to Do About It.* Addison-Wesley, 1990.

NOTES

INTRODUCTION

1. Jay Giedd, "Foreword," in Michael J. Bradley, *Yes, Your Teen Is Crazy!: Loving Your Kid Without Losing Your Mind*. Gig Harbor, WA: Harbor Press, 2002.

CHAPTER ONE

1. J.M. Twenge, et al, "Birth Cohort Increases in Psychopathology Among Young Americans, 1938–2007: A Cross-Temporal Meta-Analysis of the MMPI." *Clinical Psychology Review* 30(2), March, 2010, 145–154.
2. J.M. Twenge, et al, "It's Beyond My Control: A Cross-Temporal Meta-Analysis of Increasing Externality in Locus of Control, 1960–2002," *Personality and Social Psychology Review* 8(3), (2004): 308–319.
3. Michele Borba, *UnSelfie: Why Empathetic Kids Succeed in Our All-About-Me World* (New York: Touchstone, 2016).

CHAPTER FIVE

1. Jacobellis v. Ohio, 378 U.S. 184 (1964).

CHAPTER SIX

1. E. T. Gershoff and A. Grogan-Kaylor, "Spanking and Child Outcomes: Old Controversies and New Meta-Analyses," *Journal of Family Psychology* 30(4) (June, 2016): 453–469.

CHAPTER SEVEN

1. Thaves, Fred, *Frank and Ernest*, United Features Syndicate (1982).
2. The National Center on Addiction and Substance Abuse, Adolescent Substance Abuse (June, 2011).
3. M. L. Prendergast, et al, "The Effectiveness of Drug Abuse Treatment: A Meta-Analysis of Comparison Group Studies," *Drug and Alcohol Dependence* 67(1) (June 1, 2002): 53–72.

CHAPTER TEN

1. Fred J. Hanna, *Therapy with Difficult Clients: Using the Precursors Model to Awaken Change.* Washington, DC: American Psychological Association (2002).

INDEX

ABOUT THE AUTHOR

Dr. Michael J. Bradley is a licensed clinical psychologist with over 30 years of experience working with adolescents. He is the award-winning author of four previous books including the bestselling *Yes, Your Teen Is Crazy!—Loving Your Kid Without Losing Your Mind.* A much sought-after speaker, Dr. Bradley's down-to-earth presentations have informed and inspired audiences around the country.

To stay up to date on current teen issues;

To request a phone consultation; or

To inquire about having Dr. Bradley speak for your school or group: go to www.doctormikebradley.com and/or like him on Facebook